HOW TO PROMOTE INDIE MUSIC

DIRECTIONS TO BUILD A COMMUNITY AROUND MEANINGFUL ARTISTRY

JON ANDERSON

TWO
STORY
MEDIA

CONTENTS

To Allison: Thanks for your consistent encouragement.

You rock.

To artists: Thanks for making music that matters. You also rock (not as much, though).

I hope you find this book helpful.

EXPECTATIONS

In 2015, late one night in the middle of November, a 13-year-old named Billie Eilish Pirate Baird O'Connell uploaded a song to SoundCloud. It was called "Ocean Eyes.

The chill-pop track was the definition of bedroom art, and, like most bedroom art, it had been created with limited aspiration for finding an audience outside of friends and family. Billie's brother, Finneas, had originally written and produced the song (in his bedroom, obviously) for the use of his own band, but he ended up giving it to his sister, instead, who added the vocals. Billie herself first intended to use it as the basis for a routine she was working on with her dance teacher. It reached the internet only because she wanted her teacher to be able to access the song as they choreographed the piece.

She went to sleep and the track blew up — literally, overnight.

"Finneas called, like, 'Dude! Our song got 1,000 plays. We made it,'" Billie told *Vogue*[1]. "And then it just kept going... I didn't realize how big it was getting until it had reached 50,000 plays."

The momentum was driven by a combination of algorithmic luck and the fact that the song was undeniably head-turning. The juxtaposition of Billie's haunting, innocent soprano delivering apocalyptic lyrics ("burning cities and napalm skies") over minimalist percussion and ambient synths first caught the ear of *Hillydilly*, a taste-making blog and SoundCloud aggregator, who called the song "all it takes for a career to be set" in a sparkling two-paragraph review. From there, the plays kept coming.

It wasn't long before the track had racked up hundreds of thousands of streams. The virality immediately piqued the interest of LA-based manager Danny Rukasin.

"Ocean Eyes drove all of us to take notice," remembers Rukasin[2]. "The next day I was with [Finneas] and his family and with Billie, meeting everybody and talking about what they wanted to do. The song had already crossed into viral territory overnight."

The scenario was any artist's dream. Following quick deliberations, Billie was signed by Rukasin and partner Brandon Goodman. Under their management, she was added to the roster at Darkroom (under Interscope), which re-released "Ocean Eyes" a year later in 2016 to massive digital success and a generally favorable critical reception.

The track had momentum. The team was in place. Top 40 airplay seemed a cinch. And then Eilish stopped — or, rather, the promo did.

Her team paused the mainstream push, opting to forgo radio play. Without it, the song peaked at 84 on the Billboard US

Hot 100, and while a series of remixes would be released later, it's clear that the song underperformed its commercial potential as a result of intentional promotional underselling — maybe even promotional dampening.

Why?

On first take, the promotional approach that Billie Eilish's team took with "Ocean Eyes" is insane. It actually seems to run counter to the whole point of having a label and a team to manage music. For most aspiring artists — whose efforts are focused toward the entirely opposite objective of maximizing plays — achieving the dream of Top 40 airplay is what it means to arrive. The idea of holding back publicity at that stage is equivalent to taking a seat after 26.1 miles of a marathon.

A *New York Times* profile[3] published in support of Eilish's eventual full-length debut album (delivered three years later) provides an interesting bit of insight into the method behind the madness.

> Instead of pushing "Ocean Eyes," which goes down easy as vaguely R&B indie-pop, to Top 40 radio, Eilish's team vowed to move slower and more deliberately. "We didn't want it to be about a song," said (Brandon) Goodman, who with Danny Rukasin manages Eilish and Finneas. "We never wanted anything to be bigger than Billie the artist."

"We never wanted anything to be bigger than Billie the artist."

If that was the goal, Billie's team succeeded.

"Ocean Eyes" was inarguably a viral track. It founded a fanbase and launched the career of a global pop icon. And yet Billie

Eilish's first breakthrough megahit is currently her *10th-most-streamed song to date.*

How is that possible?

In other words, how has Billie Eilish been able to achieve such sustained, consistent success in an industry littered with one-hit wonders? How can she release a 14-track LP mixed with disparate genres and styles but have every single song notch streams in the tens of millions (with the majority reaching hundreds of millions of plays)?

The answer, I think, is the key to making music for a living. It's one that's common to any successful musician — from global icons like Taylor Swift to indie survivors like Sleeping at Last. It's the reason why artists have fans. And it's simple in concept but complex in application.

It's this: Billie Eilish has built a community.

THE PROBLEM

This is a book about music promotion. Before we get any further, we need to answer two burning questions: First, what is music promotion? And second, why do so many artists hate it?

Here are my answers — and they're related, unsurprisingly. Music promotion is the act of building a strong community around meaningful music.

So many artists hate it because they misunderstand what it is.

Far from seeing it as something meaningful, they think it's something close to a collection of underhanded used car sales tactics.

We need a perspective shift.

We need to view music promotion the way Billie Eilish's team did — the way all successful artists and teams do — not as the means to push a product, but as a means to build a community.

Unfortunately, if you're like most indie artists, your experience releasing music doesn't mirror Billie's.

Here's how it goes instead: You put countless hours and tons of effort and maybe your firstborn child's soul into a song. You work it through recording, production, mixing, mastering. You freaking love it (or at least you can tolerate it by the time it's finished). You arbitrarily mark up a release date, post the news on your socials, and get overly hyped. You send the track to your distributor and wait in eager anticipation for the day to arrive. Finally, release day comes, and...

Crickets.

Maybe you get a few thousand plays. Maybe you get a congratulatory text from your mom. But you certainly don't get hundreds of thousands of plays overnight. And then, a week after your song is out, you realize that nobody's really going to hear it. You check your Spotify Artist stats and see one playlist save.

It was you. You saved your song to your own playlist.

If you aren't Billie Eilish, you know that releasing and promoting music can kind of suck. It can give you that same sad feeling you had when you were twelve and you invited the whole class to your birthday party and nobody came. It can give you the feeling that you don't have a community.

Here's the unfortunate truth: You may *not* have a valuable community. You may not see a path to building one.

I've found that you're more likely to view the world this way if you are seeking to create what you believe is *meaningful* music — music with depth. In a world where so many of the tactics being espoused by marketers seem empty at best and scammy at worst, to self-promote feels like a soul-sucking grind.

You don't want to message a bunch of people you know on Instagram, telling them to check out your new song, only to get unfollowed by half your friends. You don't want to spend five hours researching and submitting to the "perfect" blogs only to hear nothing in response. You don't want to spend a few hundred bucks on Facebook ads and end up with nothing but an empty wallet, three followers from Faketown, and a burning feeling of regret.

You want to be an artist, not a used car salesman.

Because of this, you probably find that you put a ton of effort into making your music but then shortchange yourself when it comes time to put the music out into the world. You might shoot out a few social media posts or request coverage from a blog or two, but you likely stop before you get anywhere that makes a difference.

I've interviewed hundreds of artists at *Two Story Melody*, and I hear similar themes from them over and over again.

I recently spoke with an artist named Joel about his songwriting on a new album. Joel's put out a decent catalogue of music; the album I talked about with him is his second full-length. He's unsigned, but he's raised over $50,000 on Kickstarter to fund his work so far. It's pretty obvious he has an engaged community. His music is meaningful, and from a numbers perspective, it has traction — all 12 songs from his first album notched over 500,000 streams on Spotify. His top tracks have over a million plays.

But I was struck by his perception that he wasn't doing promotion well.

"Promo is just a grind," he told me. "I spend so much time and effort on the music, and when I release it I already feel worn out. I think my last album could've done better if I'd done a better job of promoting it."

If you're like Joel — if you're like most artists — you can't shake the feeling that you could be doing more to promote your music, but you feel burnt out at the same time.

Here's the truth: Promotion should be fulfilling.

Promotion is not tricking people into listening to your music. It's connecting you to people who will care about your artistry. Promotion is community building — and that's edifying, not emptying. It takes consistency, but it should not feel like a soul-sucking grind. It should feel like the difficult but good work of building a relationship.

I know that sounds great in theory. But in practice, can you really build a meaningful community around your music?

This is obviously a rhetorical question. Of course it's *possible* — Billie Eilish exists, after all. So do all of your favorite artists (unless you're a Gorillaz fan). So did the Beatles (although Paul's probably fake). But the successful communities that others have created often look like luck from the outside. Eilish went viral without really trying. Is that what promotion looks like? Do you just get discovered — or ignored?

In fairness, the answer is: sometimes. But the better answer is that, while there is a degree of randomness to success, you can intentionally create a strong community around meaningful music if you do it intelligently and authentically.

When you're making good music and you know how to promote it, you can create a community that actually cares about your music; that *appreciates* it; that *identifies* with it; that *acts* to support it. And you can start doing the thing all indie artists since the dawn of time (or at least the internet) have wanted to do: make a living making meaningful music — and more importantly, connecting with people in a meaningful way.

This book exists to help you get there.

2

THE BACKGROUND

As we dive in, I'd like to offer more context for this book to help delineate where it fits into the music-business-book landscape (which is huge, and probably growing as you read this).

Importantly, this book is *not* about the fundamentals of the music business. We won't be working through picking a distributor, getting set up on SoundExchange, collecting royalties, and other stuff like that. I'd recommend Ari Herstand's *How to Make It in the New Music Business* or Donald Passman's *All You Need to Know About the Music Business* for music business advice. We're covering how to promote music. It's related to business — it's a part of the bigger picture — but we'll keep our focus granular.

This is also not an encyclopedia. I've read a fair number of books positioned similarly (or at least titled similarly) to this one that attempt to offer artists explanations on every platform and tactic under the sun: Here's what TikTok is and here's how to use it. Here's what Facebook is and here are a few thoughts on how to grow an audience there. Here's how to set up pre-roll ads on YouTube. Et cetera and so on.

I think that approach is helpful if you know what you want — you can just use your encyclopedia to thumb to the tactic you're thinking of. But I think it's kind of overwhelming if you're not sure what your outcome should be, like giving you a huge LEGO kit of thousands of randomly assorted pieces and saying, "Have at it!" Yeah, everything's there, but it'll be hard to make something you're proud of. You don't need every tactic. You just need the ones that will help you accomplish your goals. If we're sticking with the LEGO analogy: You need the directions.

This book is meant to be the directions. So, while it will cover many of the platforms listed above, it won't cover *every* promotional tactic. It'll cover only the ones that I've found to be most effective in helping indie artists create engaged fans. And it'll cover them sequentially. In other words, if you follow these steps in order, assuming you're starting from the right place, you will build success.

With that said, the same directions can't work for everyone. They're only valuable if they guide you toward what *you're* trying to make or toward where *you're* trying to go — if they help you reach *your* goals.

If you're an upcoming artist who hasn't cracked the marketing code but who's willing to work hard at something worthwhile, this book is for you. If your goal is to use promotion to build a strong community around your own meaningful artistry, this book will help you get there.

It's ordered in three sections. The first will give you a framework to think about promotion. I'll walk through the four pillars of community and the three elements of artistry that undergird all good promotional efforts, then provide some exercises that will help you apply these things to your own work. By the end of the section, you'll be able to think more clearly about what effective promotion looks like and what your goals should be as an artist.

In the second section, I'll review the tools you'll need to lay a foundation that will make community building easier. We'll work through how the framework we've built applies to setting up your artist platforms before you begin any campaign. By the end of this section, you'll have your website, streaming platforms, and social channels optimized to make promotion more effective.

The third section will build from the first two to give you a straightforward path to follow when you release music. I'll provide you with a simple plan and a selection of straightforward tactics you can implement on each promotional platform. This section will equip you to release and promote your music strategically.

Altogether, the outcome should be a steadily growing community. You will grow engaged fans across the platforms that matter, solicit solid press coverage that validates your work, and unlock the potential for increased income through touring and merch sales — but, ultimately, I want this book to lead to meaningful relationships built around you and your music.

Why should your goal in promotion be to build a strong community?

To answer that question, I'll have to define my terms. Let's take a look at what a strong community is to uncover the principles behind all successful indie artistry.

It's time to lay the framework for promotion.

SECTION I

The Framework

3

THE WHAT AND WHY OF COMMUNITY

C ommunity is a nebulous word, which means, of course, that there have been plenty of attempts to nail it down. Out of all of them, the definition I like most comes from an often-cited 2001 study in the *American Journal of Public Health*[1], in which researchers used cluster analysis to review verbatim responses to the question, "What does community mean to you?" across four distinct social groups: gay men in San Francisco, injection drug users in Philadelphia, HIV vaccine researchers in the United States, and Black people in Durham.

Here's the answer they uncovered:

A community is a group of people with diverse characteristics who are linked by social ties, share common perspectives, and engage in joint action in geographical locations or settings.

This sums things up nicely. There are four main elements that define any group as a community: social ties, shared perspectives, shared settings, and shared actions. These are all that's needed to create a strong community.

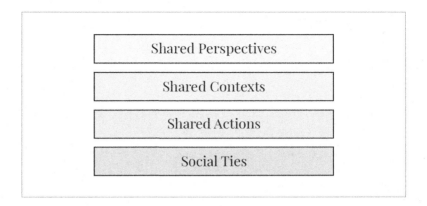

These are the pillars. Let's unpack them as they apply to communities created around artists.

Social Ties

This is the part of community that's most difficult to directly create as an indie artist, so I won't spend as much time on it here or in the pages that follow as I will on the other three pillars. With that said, there are some important things to point out.

First, a definition: Social ties are relationships between members of a group.

They're friendships.

Again (unfortunately), you can't make people interact and form relationships around your music. You can't make your fans be friends with each other. But friendships are critical components of a strong community.

The good news is that you can intentionally create the other three components of a community — and if those are in place, social ties get built naturally. Common perspectives, shared context, and joint actions lead to friendships. Focus on building a foundation of these components and fan friendships will follow.

The second point to keep in mind is that the people who have built friendships around your music will almost always be your biggest fans. You should focus on engaging these people more than you focus on any other group — in fact, over the long-term, 80% of your promotion should be focused on these people. Not only will they appreciate it, but it will also strengthen their social ties around your artistry — and, in turn, it will strengthen the ties of your community.

You can't create social ties directly, but when they're built, you should pay attention.

Common Perspectives

Perspective, on the other hand, you *can* directly impact. You get to shape this.

A community shares common perspectives on things. If you're a Taylor Swift fan, you know she told the truth about that Kanye call. (If you're a Kanye fan, you're probably pretty confused about a lot of things.) Beyond surface-level perspectives, though, the strongest communities also share perspectives on deeper-level values: They believe similar things about what matters and how the world should be.

A church is an easy example of a community built on strong shared perspectives. A political party is another. In any context, you'll notice that the strongest communities have the most clearly defined perspectives. People can easily identify what a strong community stands for and decide whether or not they feel the group's values are worth sharing.

I'll use the terms values and perspectives somewhat interchangeably because both serve the same purpose in community building, but I want to point out that there are subtle differences. Values are core beliefs. Perspectives are opinions. They're more fluid — they can change more quickly as new information is gathered, and they're often based on and shaped by values. For instance, if you value humor, you might have a favorable perspective on Post Malone. If you value responsibility, you might not. If Post Malone started a philanthropic foundation for underprivileged youth in inner cities, your perspective on him might change, but your core values wouldn't.

In marketing terms, when taken together, your values, perspectives, and the traits they lead to are your brand. But instead of using the word "brand", I like to group these things together under the word "perspective." I prefer this mostly because communities are built around beliefs more than brands (which are more general). I also prefer it because brand is a word that's been overused to the point of becoming nonsense.

Back to the point: It's easier to build a community around perspectives that are obvious.

Noname, the Chicago-based rapper who's collaborated with Chance the Rapper and beefed with J Cole, is a good example of this. Her perspective is exceptionally clear. She's risen to prominence as a notable voice on race and gender issues, with *NPR* calling her album *Room 25* "sharp commentary on race, identity, sex and politics" and "one of the most critically-acclaimed records of [2018]".[2] *NME* called her "Probably one of the most political rappers of a generation," and credited her with "using her worldwide reach to highlight current injustices still practiced today."[3]

She stands for something. And because she has a clearly defined perspective, her community is actively engaged with her. She has millions of followers, and scores of them rushed to her defense when J Cole seemingly dissed the tone of her activism in "Snow on Tha Bluff".

Her perspective also allowed her to respond quickly to that diss — within a day — by releasing "Song 33", a track that garnered wide critical acclaim (although she later expressed regret for the distraction it caused from the issues she supports). It racked up over three million Spotify streams in a little over a month.

The lesson here is that clearly expressed perspectives build community and lead to actions — for artists and their fans.

And, as Noname's quick response illustrates, having a defined perspective will help you to make decisions. For example, if you've defined loyalty as a core value, you'll find it easier to dismiss appealing opportunities that exclude people you're close to. If you value integrity, you'll be able to act quickly to pursue means of self-expression that are consistent with your beliefs. If you're Post Malone, it's an easy call to endorse Bud Light. You get the idea.

Obviously, not every successful artist has taken the time to explicitly define their perspective. But every artist that lasts — every artist that's been able to build a sustainable community — has leaned into their perspectives whether they've codified them or not. Think of any of your favorite artists and you can probably identify almost instantly what they stand for and what it means to be a fan of them.

You like Bruce Springsteen because he's relatable, hardworking, and fun.

You like Noname because she's courageous and honest.

You like Imagine Dragons because you have bad taste. (Kidding.)

It's worth observing that your perspectives and values as an artist won't be static. People grow and change, and plenty of artists have shapeshifted over the course of their careers. That's as it should be, but you have to balance authenticity with consistency. Your core values shouldn't change on a whim; if they do, they aren't core values. At the same time, if, after careful reflection, your values have changed, it's dishonest to hide that fact. However, be aware that changing your perspective significantly can alienate your community.

One cautionary tale comes from the realm of Christian music (a space where community is obviously built around shared perspective). As the lead singer of Caedmon's Call and later as a solo artist, Derek Webb was a successful act in the genre for parts of three decades. He built a community that was drawn to his thoughtful and honest expression of his faith — but, in the middle of the 2010s, he gradually realized that he no longer believed what he was singing about. In 2017, he released an album that effectively announced his transition to atheism.

Webb called the result, *Fingers Crossed,* "the story of two deeply personal divorces," (he'd separated from his wife around the same time), noting that "the job of an artist is to look at the world and describe it."

> "The challenge is whether or not you lie about what you see
> or you tell the truth. And for me, if this record was not

desperately sad, it would have been completely dishonest...
You change, the world changes, but [the process] for me has
been the same."[4]

The vast majority of his fan base was crushed. Many stopped
listening; all of the vanity metrics around his new releases
(streams, views, plays) pale in comparison to the metrics from
his previous efforts.

A subsection of his community continues to be his fans — those
who were more drawn to his values of honesty and thoughtful-
ness than to his perspective on faith — and he's picked up a
steadily growing contingent of people who identify with his
new (still clearly defined) perspectives. Webb would probably
say that his core values haven't changed. But there's no denying
the fact that drastically changing his perspective has effectively
erased the first community he'd built and made promoting his
music more difficult.

The point is this: Be highly intentional about the values you
choose to portray, and be highly intentional if you choose to
change them. You can (and should) change the *focus* of your
perspective from project to project, but always clearly define
your underlying values. Artists with easy-to-identify perspectives have an easier time building community, and the communities they build tend to have stronger connections.

Be careful about what you stand for. But stand for something.

Shared Context

A community grows around a shared context.

The *American Journal of Public Health* study, crafted in the
realm of public health, called this component of community

"shared settings". In the realm of public health, the word "setting" makes sense. The heart of the principle it refers to, though, can be boiled down to the following: Communities grow around things. In other words, communities need a context.

You can observe any community you've been a part of and easily identify its shared context. Maybe you developed a community around the context of a sports team. Maybe you built one around band camp. Maybe you joined a weird subreddit. There are limitless examples. The point is this: Any *thing* that facilitates shared experiences, shared perspectives, and shared actions is a context for community.

Your music should be a context that your community shares. All of your promotional materials and platforms can be, too. But here's the most important thing to remember about this pillar: *You, as an artist, should be your community's primary context.* Flipping the priority of your contexts (putting a piece of art above yourself as the artist) is one of the biggest mistakes in music promotion.

This mistake is exactly what Billie Eilish's team was so intent to avoid with "Ocean Eyes", and it's why underselling the song's reach was such a brilliant promotional strategy. The track could have been a primary context, but Eilish made sure that it was secondary to herself. She dampened its promotion until she had greater context built around her artistry. Instead of pushing the single, she spent time creating more clearly defined perspectives, developing more obvious branding, and making more music.

To illustrate what it means to take the opposite approach, let's look at the biggest hit of the past decade: "Old Town Road". For every Billie Eilish, there's a Lil Nas X.

More artists are hoping to make an "Old Town Road" than are working on a *When We All Fall Asleep, Where Do We Go?*. It makes sense. "Old Town Road" is one of the biggest songs ever. It spent 17 weeks at the top of the Billboard Hot 100 — an all-time record. It's responsible for the three highest weekly streaming totals in the history of digital music. The song is objectively awesome.

But here's the thing: "Old Town Road" will always be bigger than Lil Nas X.

It was hugely over-promoted. All of the promotion worked. There are four official audio versions — you probably like the one with Billy Ray Cyrus best — and four different videos. Each did incredibly well and racked up, at the very least, tens of millions of plays. There was serious work behind all of this; when the song initially went viral thanks to TikTok, Lil Nas X was quickly snapped up by Columbia Records. They certainly made sure to capitalize on his moment.

And that's fine. Lil Nas X has a million-watt smile, a golden personality, and enough momentum from one song to sustain his career for years. He and his team are working to build up his context as an artist now, and they're doing a nice job. His follow-up EP did well. His brand (built on emojis and Gen Z internet culture) is being backfilled in the wake of his meteoric rise; it still suits him.

But if you ask your mom who "Old Town Road" is by, she'll know the song — but she won't know who Lil Nas X is. His community is built around the context of "Old Town Road" more than it's built around him. He will never make a song that comes close to his previous success.

When you make a song that sits at number one for 17 weeks, that's okay. But if *you* want to have a sustainable career — if you want to create music on an ongoing basis and have it continue to matter — you should focus on building your context as an artist more than you prioritize any single piece of art. Billie Eilish will be making hits for longer than Lil Nas X, and she'll be remembered as an icon. Lil Nas X will be remembered as the guy who made "Old Town Road", a fact his brand readily acknowledges.

If you want sustainable success, don't promote your art. Promote your artistry.

Much of this book will carry out the practical ramifications of this idea, but I'll set the stage with a few final thoughts.

First, to promote your artistry, you have to have a clearly defined artist perspective that transcends a single piece of your art. In other words, every piece of art or promotional platform should support your perspective as an artist. Nas did the opposite. "Old Town Road" doesn't support his perspective; he had to align his perspective to fit the track.

> (Nas) wasn't too familiar with cowboy culture: While he'd worn Wranglers growing up ("It's Georgia, everybody wore Wranglers"), he had to Google other Western lingo. He chose the title "Old Town Road" because "it sounded like a real country place. I was surprised it hadn't been used before."[5]

"Old Town Road" is a great context for community. But because it's been emphasized over Lil Nas X, it's become a barrier that will make it hard for him to stop wearing cowboy hats.

Billie Eilish's biggest hit to date is "bad guy". It's based on values that support Eilish's artist persona. Instead of confining her, it lays a foundation for her perspectives to be expressed in evolving ways.

The takeaway is to make sure you clarify what you stand for before you start promoting something.

Second, the more art you create, the more context you'll have supporting your artistry. This is why Eilish's team intentionally undersold "Ocean Eyes" — so that they could focus on creating more art (and more context) that supported Billie Eilish the artist. It's also why Lil Nas X was vulnerable to becoming a one-hit-wonder — he'd only been making music for a year and had no other context built up around him when "Old Town Road" blew up. As a result, his team was quick to follow up the hit with an EP.

The truth is that if someone saves your song, they're not your fan; they're a fan of your song. If they buy your entire catalogue, they're a fan of you. Lasting communities are built around artists. So before you over-promote, create enough context to make fandom of your artistry possible.

Focus on the catalogue, not the quick hit.

Shared Actions

Finally, communities are strengthened by acting together.

> Fellowship is heaven, and lack of fellowship is hell; fellowship is life, and lack of fellowship is death; and the deeds that ye do upon the earth, it is for fellowship's sake ye do them.[6]

I love this quote; although it's taken far outside of its intended (19th-century-socialistic) context, the point stands. Not only does action build community, but community also drives action. When we do something, we're doing it with others in mind. When we act in public, we almost always act for others.

Communities and actions are deeply intertwined.

You can look at any community you've been part of and identify its shared actions. The act of practicing together as a band day after day in the heat of summer is a big part of why there are so many stories from band camp. The military puts people through bootcamp partly to train skills, but, just as importantly, to build camaraderie and commitment. The LGBTQ community hosts parades to express its perspective, but also to make its community participatory — when you march together, you belong together.

Shared actions are the most emotionally impactful part of community building. This is why joining an exclusive community often requires some kind of initiation. When people act with a group, they will be more invested in it. Action is the biggest signal of commitment. Weddings involve buying and giving rings, not just saying words.

As an artist, one of your goals in promotion should be to lead your community in actions that align with your perspective and help to create your context. There are obvious actions that your fans can take to support you: signing up for your email list, buying your merch, or attending a show. You should also get creative. Good promotion creates unique opportunities to act in support of an artist community.

For example, Sleeping At Last (the soft-indie-rock brainchild of Ryan O'Neal) completed a project based on a personality typing system called the Enneagram. According to the Enneagram, there are nine personality types; O'Neal recorded a song based on each one. For every track, he asked fans who identified as that personality type to record a noise that they felt represented their type's meaning and send it to him. He then collected all of those noises and used them to build the sonic textures of the songs.

O'Neal's idea was artsy and imbued meaning to his work, but its greatest value was in giving his community a unique action to take that aligned perfectly with O'Neal's perspective as an artist. If you sent in a noise, you would certainly follow the project — and, better yet, you'd feel like a part of it.

Like O'Neal, you should find unique actions to encourage that align with your artistry. Don't be afraid to ask for big things. Generally, the more an action *costs* (in time, money, or effort), the larger the commitment it signals. The person who signs up for your email list is a fan. The person who attends every one of your shows this year is a superfan. Provide people with options to test the waters, but also give them options to deeply commit.

One final point on shared action: People are more likely to act when others are acting, too.

This is the reason people stop and look for the source of excitement when they see a crowd gathered, a fact that any experienced street performer understands and takes advantage of. The presence of others acting makes action seem more appealing. The French philosopher Le Bon articulated this phenomenon as contagion theory, and it's pretty simple: Crowds incite participation.

So, just like street performers construct crowds or seed their instrument cases with tips, you should consider building the appearance of shared action so that others will be inspired to stop and pay attention. While I usually disparage vanity metrics, this is the area where they can actually help. Use things like Facebook likes and streaming numbers to create the sense of collective action. As I've noted before, these metrics have some value in themselves, but their bigger value is in the actions they can encourage.

Actions build community only when people act together. Create opportunities for shared actions to support your artistry.

4

WHY COMMUNITY MATTERS

N ow you know what a strong community is: a group linked by social ties, common perspectives, shared context, and shared actions.

There are two reasons why it matters.

First, the creation of and participation in a strong community is what every artist — and person — most wants.

Second, strong communities are more economically viable than large communities that aren't strong.

Those are big claims, I know. But they're true.

The Fulfillment Justification for a Strong Community

Strong communities offer the two things that every person desires most deeply: a sense of belonging and a sense of participation in something bigger than yourself.

Let's cover belonging, first. Maslow's Hierarchy of Needs[1] lists love and belonging right above physical safety. In other words, after your physical needs are satisfied, Maslow believes that the next most pressing requirement you have as a person is to be accepted. But you don't need Maslow to tell you what you already know: In the deepest levels of your being, you want to belong.

You want a strong community.

Humans are social creatures. In every framework for human behavior — evolutionary, psychological, sociological, spiritual, et. all — the constant and unavoidable conclusion is that people thrive in relationships. People need groups.

Artists know this, maybe better than anyone. In the words of eden ahbez (as sung by legends like Nat Cole, David Bowie, and Ewan McGregor), "The greatest thing you'll ever learn is just to love, and be loved in return." That's the core of living well, and it's only offered in relationship to others — in community.

Second, strong communities offer participation in a cause bigger than yourself. You need this, too. Maslow might categorize this desire under "self actualization," but I like David Brook's description of the "second mountain" better.

Brooks posits that people seek personal achievement first; in other words, early in life, we live to get acclaim for ourselves — to collect things like awards or monumental shows or money that we think will bring us satisfaction. But he believes that when we do achieve personal acclaim, we realize that it isn't truly fulfilling. The pursuit of individual satisfaction isn't ultimately satisfying. So, next, we turn from seeking *personal* acclaim and move toward supporting something *outside* of us:

in our framework, a community. Brooks calls this new pursuit "the second mountain," and argues that it's far more satisfying than pursuing personal acclaim.[2] Along with cultivating belonging, I believe that pursuing a second mountain is a key to living well.

Your community can give you both a sense of belonging and a sense of commitment to something bigger than yourself. It can give you joy. And it can give other people those things, too.

To clarify, I don't believe that your artist community should be your core identity. Even strong communities fade. But I do think that your community can be a service to you and to others by facilitating belonging and participation in a cause that's bigger than you. Because even though you are building community around your artistry, it's about more than your achievement or acclaim or money. It's about connection.

Since I read it as a kid, I've been haunted by the end of *Into the Wild*, Jon Krakauer's 1996 book chronicling the true story of Chris McCandless (or, as he preferred to call himself, Alexander Supertramp)[3]. McCandless was a wanderer; disenchanted with the emptiness of American society, he dropped out of it altogether and hitchhiked his way alone through a series of adventures, never lingering in one place long enough to develop lasting relationships. At 24, he found himself living in remote reaches of the Alaskan wilderness. It was there, miles away from the nearest human and living in the wreck of a van, that he became fatally ill after accidentally eating poisonous berries.

As he died alone, McCandless — the supertramp who'd left everyone behind to find himself — wrote the devastating truth in his journal.

"Happiness is only real when shared."

In the end, connection is what everything comes back to. Build it. If you don't, you'll be haunted by it.

The Economic Justification for a Strong Community

The second reason to pursue a strong community is because it is valuable. A strong community will allow you to make music for a living.

Unfortunately, while most artists do want to build a community (even if they don't fully understand what that means), most are chasing community size more than community strength.

Community size is portrayed in vanity metrics — things like numbers of streams, numbers of likes, and numbers of views. These are easy to measure (which is part of why they're appealing to pursue), but they're only one factor in a community's economic value, and they often don't correlate to economic viability.

There are plenty of artists with millions of Spotify streams that have trouble putting food on the table. These artists might have gotten included on an editorial playlist, racked up the plays, and gotten a decent check, but unless they've built a community through those means, the monetary success will fade when the playlist is updated. As you've probably seen, a lot of artists with millions of plays have trouble selling out a hundred-person venue.

Community strength is the more important economic factor. Strength is built on the pillars we've listed in our definition (which, you'll notice, doesn't include community size).

Unfortunately, the presence of social ties and shared perspectives, context, and actions are more difficult to measure than vanity metrics. But observations like retention rate (how long people remain a part of the community), engagement rate (how likely people are to act in support of a community), and average fan spend represent these elements to some degree.

To illustrate why strong communities are economically viable, it's helpful to break the concept of community down into a simple equation that accounts for the two main variables in an artist's economic success: the size of their audience (X) and the average amount each of their fans spends (Y) — a shared action that's positively correlated to community strength. XY will equal artist income (Z).

$$X \times Y = Z$$

| Audience size | Average fan spend | Artist income |

Here's how that plays out over a few data points.

Number of Fans	Average Annual Fan Spend	Annual Income
1,000	$100	$100,000
10,000	$10	$100,000
100,000	$1	$100,000
1,000,000	$0.1	$100,000
10,000,000	$.01	$100,000
100,000,000	$.001	$100,000

Both variables have an equally weighted impact on income, but the average spend of a fan is worth prioritizing in your promotional efforts for two reasons: first, because it requires less change at a gross level, making it easier to impact; going from $1 to $10 in fan spend requires less effort than going from 10,000 to 100,000 fans. Second, because it's easier to maintain; if 100,000,000 fans are only spending $.001 (roughly equivalent to payment for one Spotify stream), they're hardly fans, and they probably won't follow your music unless it's force-fed to them. Maintaining success with a huge audience at low engagement levels will require consistent over-promotion of the kind that'll leave you feeling empty and tired.

On the other hand, if someone is spending $100 of their money to buy merch and see a show, they're committed. They'll probably seek out everything you release, year after year. You will have to consistently produce art that they'll value, but making good art is inherently more fulfilling and sustainable.

This equation is, more or less, the foundation for Kevin Kelly's "1,000 True Fans" concept[4] — the idea that artists can achieve economic success with only 1,000 fans spending, on average, $100 each year.

This idea has been repeated ad nauseum, but there are plenty of caveats to it that make it somewhat misleading. Maybe most importantly, while Kelly himself was concerned with profit, most references to his idea tie the metrics to gross income instead — so they don't account for the cost of goods sold or other fees. For example, if a fan buys a $20 t-shirt that costs you $10 to print and ship, you've only made a profit of $10. If tickets cost $20, but your cut, for simplicity's sake, is 50%, you only make $10. The reality is that artists who make $100,000 in gross sales are only bringing home a fraction of that income after fees and taxes. It's also worth noting that almost nobody spends $100 on a single artist every year, so finding 1,000 people willing to do this is harder than it sounds.

On the flip side, we also haven't accounted for additional sources of income that aren't dependent on fans, like sync licensing.

With all of this said, a career in music tends to realistically land somewhere not shown in the simple data points of our chart; the metrics I've seen suggest that to make a decent middle-class income, you need at least 10,000 fans spending in the vicinity of $20 on your music each year[5]. That's not as catchy as having 1,000 true fans, but it's definitely attainable.

That's the economic benefit to focusing on building community strength over vanity metrics. A strong community is more valuable.

5

THE FOUNDATIONS OF ARTISTRY

Up till this point, I've written about your community: what it is, what it should be, and why it matters. Now, it's time to shift gears and talk about you. The success of your promotion — the strength of your community — is largely dependent on the quality of your artistry.

This is the part where I tell you the secret to success in the music industry.

I'm kidding. I'm not that arrogant, at least about that. (I *am* better than you at ping-pong.) Anyway, this isn't a secret; it's just common sense. You already know these things, but let's put language to them. While a community is built on four pillars, there are three elements to successful individual artistry: *consistency*, *connection*, and *competency*.

I view these three components as the three legs of a stool. They're interconnected; you need all three to have a sustainable career. If one isn't working, your music won't work for you in the long run. If your music isn't working, one of these things is broken.

So, let's break them down.

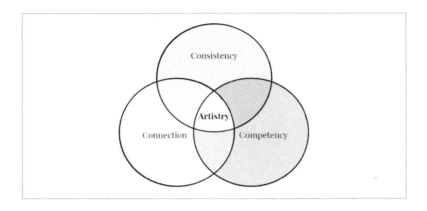

Consistency

Consistency matters in two ways. First, and most obviously, you've got to consistently work to improve your abilities. Like my seventh grade basketball coach used to say, "Hard work beats talent when talent doesn't work hard." (I always felt like that was a putdown, for some reason, but maybe that's a personal issue.)

But second (and this is the crux of this point), you've got to consistently make, release, and play music.

Artist consistency is what builds the community pillar of context. Daniel Ek, the CEO of Spotify, took a lot of flak this year for suggesting that "you can't record music once every three to four years and think that's going to be enough."[1] Artists hated that statement, but the truth is that he's right. If you're trying to make it, you've got to make music — again and again and again. This is something that's even more important in today's noisy music landscape than it was 20 years ago, and it's something not enough artists take seriously. Too many indie artists put out one album and then tour it and then don't put anything out for a couple of years. Or, worse, they put out one *song* and then wait for a couple of years.

Look, I know making music is time-consuming, and I know that you want to get tracks right before you put them out. But if you truly want to be an artist, you have to recognize that a key to building momentum is to continually have music to build momentum on. One release is basically a shout into the void; even if everything works spectacularly, it'll fade within the year, and your fans will stop tracking with you. Consistent releases are a conversation that builds context. Your fans will keep coming back because they'll want to check up on what you're doing.

This applies to pretty much every aspect of musicianship and every creative endeavor. The best artists usually make a lot of art. Most things that are worthwhile were built consistently over a long period of time. You know, like that whole thing about Rome. It wasn't built in a day, but they were laying bricks every hour.

There are a lot of ways to maintain consistency, and the tack you'll take will largely be determined by your goals and desires. But it's essential to shift your perspective away from trying to "make it" and toward making music consistently. Artistry is a journey, not a destination. If you treat each project like a desti-nation, you'll be in danger of emphasizing your art over your artistry. Enjoy each project as a step. At times, you should reflect on where you've come from and enjoy what you've made. But never lose sight of the fact that you are a continual creator.

Here are a few ideas to practically shift your mindset and output toward consistency.

- Record twelve tracks every year. Batch your production so that it all happens at once.
- Release half of your tracks as singles — one each month for five or six months — so that you can have a consistent stream of new music.
- Do more than one release show. Play consistently throughout the year. (In other words, tour, often.)
- Commit to consistent promotion. Instead of posting once a month on Instagram, post three times a week. Instead of writing once every two years on your blog, do a weekly blog post about your process.
- Set a goal to write a certain number of songs every month.

If you want to make a living making music, treat it like a job and do it every day. It's work, but it's worth it. Because you and I both know that making music is an awesome job.

Connection

In using the word "connection" here, I don't necessarily mean the kind of connection that builds a community; I mean the kind of connection that'll get you ahead. This is one part of promotion that it's easy to feel jaded by. Yeah, the people who are good at promotion always have connections.

Let's face it: Some people have an advantage in this from birth. They're born into a rich family that plugs them into connections right away. Or they just happen to know somebody who can give them the big break — that chance to open for a big act or to work with that one producer.

The thing to remember, though, is that even though some people start from ahead, *you can intentionally choose to connect.* Actually, in today's world, where everyone's contact info is creepily available online, the head starts are less important because you've got more opportunities for developing connections than ever before. It'll just take you more work if you don't personally know Jack Antonoff.

I recommend that as you work to promote your music, you intentionally connect with two types of people.

First, connect with the people you want to emulate, even if it's just to ask for advice. What artists are doing the things you want to do? Reach out to them on social channels. Dig for their emails. Let them know you appreciate what they're doing and ask if they'd be willing to let you buy them a coffee. If they're not local (or if you're an introvert), ask a few questions over text or email.

Here's an interesting thing about humans: They want to talk about themselves. Most people want to share their stories. If you're genuinely interested in people as *people* — not as means to your ends — most of them will share. Learning people's stories can give you huge insight into what successful work in the industry looks like.

If the people you want to emulate seem too far out of reach, work a few steps down the ladder. Who's opening for the artists you want to emulate? Who's producing their stuff? Who's writing it? Who's writing with the people writing it? Being in these circles is more than a step toward bigger things — it's a community in itself.

You should list 10 of these people (who you want to emulate or who are connected with the people you want to emulate) in a document that will become your *Artist Impact List*.

Second, connect with industry people you'd like to work with. These may be some of the same people you want to emulate, but this is generally a broader circle.

One strategy here is to go to musician or artist conferences. There are a lot of them, and yeah, they can be kind of weird and networking at them can kind of suck — but they also bring together tons of awesome people into one spot and basically force you to interact.

List 10 people you'd like to work with in your *Artist Impact List*.

The bottom line in all of this is that you should find people involved with what you want to be doing and reach out to learn their stories. There doesn't have to be an end game to these interactions. Again, there probably shouldn't be. A big key to this is *not asking for anything in return*. Just get to know people and opportunities will follow. At the very least, you'll get to know more about the industry. And who knows — you might even make a few friends.

Connections matter, which is kind of lame. But you can intentionally make connections, which is cool.

Competency

I've saved the most important element of artistry for last. Here's the question that matters most: How good are you at what you do? Seriously ask yourself this. Because the artists with the best abilities rise to the top.

Now, don't get me wrong. I don't want you to start doubting yourself, and I absolutely don't want you to get paralyzed into inaction by thinking you aren't good enough. Actually, I want the opposite: I want you to be driven to action by the desire for improvement. The best artists are. They always want to get better, and they keep working so that they do.

In addition to asking *if* you're good, you also need to analyze *where* your strengths lie. What are you good at, where are you weak, and how can you improve? At some level, the answers are linked to natural ability. You might naturally be a gifted vocalist, have an innate sense of rhythm, or be blessed with an awesome ear for harmony.

But so are a lot of people. Artists today have to stand out at a national (even international) level. So, keep working.

A word of advice: Focus on honing your strengths and supplementing your weaknesses with help from others. For example, if you're confident in your vocals but know you're a mediocre guitar player, get help from session guitarists when you record and find someone who can nail live instrumentation during your shows. Yeah, keep working on improving your guitar skill, but don't let it hold you back — let other people help you push forward.

Focus on showcasing your strengths.

The bottom line here is that the artists who make it are good at what they do, whatever that is. There's something about them that stands out from the crowd and they've figured out what it is and capitalized on it. Figure out what it is for you.

With artist competency in mind, I'd like to define a term that's important in our promotional framework. I've said that promotion is only worthwhile for meaningful music; here, I'd like to clarify what I mean by "meaningful".

In the context of this book, meaningful music is any music that has the capacity to build a community.

In other words, all music can be meaningful, but different music is meaningful to different degrees. Meaningfulness is a value that exists on a spectrum. It is not a binary option.

Again, this is nearly impossible to quantify. But meaning is founded on the four pillars of community. Music is more meaningful the more clearly it defines a perspective, the more successfully it creates a shared context, the more persuasively it encourages action, and the more robustly it creates social ties.

I'll give a few examples to illustrate.

I've had a (not small) number of artists email me to express frustration that their music isn't getting covered, voicing something to this effect: "My music is awesome, but it's too intelligent and deep, and people are too lazy / disengaged / culturally blinded to get it."

This is bullshit. If people aren't connecting with your music, there are two potential issues: one, your music isn't meaningful, or, two, you aren't promoting it well. You are not the only intelligent and profound person in the world. If your music truly is meaningful, you can build a community around it.

Usually, when I listen to the work of these artists, the issue is the music. It's simply not very good; the artist's competency is the problem. It might have rough production or a bad vocal performance. Bad art is less meaningful; if Michaelangelo had painted with the same intention but less skill, nobody would have cared about his work.

If technical proficiency isn't an issue, then often the music is simply too obscure — the verses are abstractly poetic, or the point of the chorus is unclear, or the arrangement doesn't fit the theme. Music like this obviously means something to the artist, but it doesn't mean anything to anyone else. This is a competency issue, too — it's bad songwriting.

On the other end of things, you have Lady Gaga.

Lady Gaga is undeniably competent. You might not consider her music meaningful. That's fine; maybe it's not to you. It's only pop music. Melodically, it's nothing that hasn't been done before, although she's certainly got a powerful voice. And it's hard to argue that her lyrics are incredibly profound, even if they can be somewhat weird. But for the thousands of "Little Monsters" who follow her across the internet and petition for her to receive the Nobel Peace Prize — there's *something* about her music that is having a deep impact.

Lady Gaga's artistry intentionally builds on the four pillars of community. It represents her unique perspective; she wore a meat dress to protest animal cruelty. A meat dress is not music, obviously, but it represents a clearly defined perspective, for sure.

She's built deep context; she's released five studio albums, a film soundtrack, and tons of other work spanning more than a decade of artistry. She maintains an active fanclub website. She was great in *A Star Is Born*. She's prolific, and her fans understand what she stands for because of the expansive context she's created.

She incentivizes action; in tandem with her release of "Born This Way" in 2011, she created the Born This Way foundation to make mental health resources available to kids, and encouraged her fans to support the cause.

And, as a result, her fans have developed social ties and friendships around her music; littlemonsters.com offers plenty of proof of that.

Her music is meaningful because it builds a community.

What music do you consider meaningful? Even if the music you consider meaningful is eighty times more complex and artful than "Poker Face," you will be able to quickly identify how it builds on the four pillars of community to create meaning.

Here's the takeaway: Music is not meaningful because of intricate chord progressions, expert musicianship, or obscurely poetic lyrics. Those things are valuable to pursue because they can make music artistically good and *enhance* its meaning, but they aren't meaningful in themselves. Meaningful music means something to someone other than the artist. Meaningful music builds a community.

You should strive to increase your competency because you'll be able to create more meaningful music.

And that's the only thing worth promoting.

6

DOCUMENT YOUR FRAMEWORK

B y now, you understand what a community is and why it matters. You also understand what it takes to be an artist that can create a community. Now, it's time to start homing things in so that you can take practical steps to promote your music.

In this chapter, I'm going to cover how to set goals that support community building.

Right now, what are your goals as an artist?

It's such a basic question, right? But it gets me every time. It's absolutely critical to ask and answer this question if you want to promote your music well (and, really, if you want to do anything well). If you don't set goals, you'll have no idea what you're shooting for, and any actions you take will ultimately be aimless.

At this point, I've made the argument that your core goal should be to build a community around your artistry. But that's the center of the circle; start from there, and there is still infinite variety to the direction the radii can go. It's time to get more specific.

There are three things you'll need to define. First, what are your core values? These will shape your artistry. Second, what will your artist community look like? This will shape what successful promotion means for you. Third, what are your supporting goals? These will give you practical steps to take to build community.

Let's walk through these three things.

Core Values

First, define the core values that will form the basis of your artist perspective. Here's a practical exercise to help.

1. *Ask questions.*

- What are three peak experiences you've had? (Times you were fulfilled, joyful, excited.) What values were you honoring? List three.
- What are three difficult experiences you've had? (Times you were discouraged, angry, or upset.) What values were being threatened? List three.
- What are three things (other than basic necessities) that you need in your life? What values do they represent? List three.

1. *Identify themes.*

Look at all nine values you've listed and identify common themes. You should be able to boil things down into three to five words that represent your essential beliefs about what matters. These are your core values, and they should permeate everything you do as an artist (and a person). List these in a document titled *Core Values List*. Your perspectives as an artist will often flow from these.

I've found this process for determining values helpful, but it's far from the only one. No matter how you arrive at your core values, the key is to be intentional. Spend time on this. Carve out dedicated space to reflect (and maybe journal) on what matters to you.

Community Visualization

Second, identify what the community you'll build will look like. This will follow naturally from your perspective and values, to an extent — but get very practical, too. For each of the three pillars that you can impact, document what your ideal community would look like.

These questions can give you a start.

1. *Perspective*

- What things will make your community sad?
- What topics will bring your community joy?
- What causes will your community support?

1. *Context*

- In what physical places will your community gather?
- Where online will your community meet?
- At the end of your career, what will your catalogue include?

1. *Actions*

- How can your community contribute to the creation of your art?
- What will your community do to respond to your art?
- What kinds of things will your biggest fans do to identify as your biggest fans?

List the answers in a document called a *Community Visualization Plan*. As with the earlier exercise to home in on core values, these questions are only one starting point. The key, again, is to explicitly detail what your community will look like. Regardless of the exercises you use, be as specific as possible. Your vision for your community will evolve over time, but the more clearly you can define it, the better chance you'll be able to build it. You've got to see the picture on the box to be able to put the pieces of the puzzle together.

Supporting Goal Creation

With your core values defined and your community visualized, it's time to get even more tactical. What are the actual steps you will take to build the community you've envisioned?

A disclaimer: Setting supporting goals is one of the hardest parts of promoting music.

Again, the problem is that there's an unbelievable amount of noise out there. I've drawn heavily on my LEGO analogy, but what was missing from that was the social pressure to use every LEGO piece — to try every tactic. You've heard that you've got to be on SoundCloud if you're a rapper, right? Or that the best chance at going viral is on TikTok? Or that you need to be posting covers on YouTube? Or that...

Everyone has a take, and everyone's take feels so urgent. You'll eliminate a lot of the noise if you've defined your core values and your end goal — but even then, there still are limitless paths your promotion might take.

You need a system. Enter 3-2-1 goal setting.

The basic concept of a 3-2-1 *Goal Plan* is taken from Geno Wickman's *Traction,* a book of frameworks, processes, and tools that help business owners build companies that systematically set and achieve goals. It's worth a read if you're into systems; Geno compiled a bunch of stuff from other accomplished business thinkers (like John Rockefeller and Verne Harnish) and boiled it down into a framework that helps bring clarity and direction.

3-2-1 is boiled down even further and tailored to musicians. Here's how it works. Once you've identified your core values and ideal community, ask yourself three questions:

1. What are the three goals I can pursue this year that are most likely to help me create the community I envision?
2. What are the two activities I can do for each goal for the next three months that will most impact their achievement?
3. What is the one leading indicator for each activity that I can use to track my progress?

Let's make things less abstract with an example. Say you're attempting to build a community around nu-metal music. Your 3-2-1 *Goal Plan* might look like this.

Nu-Metal Community Goals		
Goal	**Reach 1M Spotify streams by the end of the year.**	**Reach 2K email subscribers by the end of the year.** · **Play live in front of 10K+ people.**
Activity	Release new music.	Create an email newsletter · Email venues to book more gigs.
Metric	# of hours spent working on new songs	# of hours spent writing · # of emails sent
Activity	Email indie playlist curators.	Set up a text-in email signup to collect emails at every show. · Connect with artists in your scene.
Metric	# of emails sent	# of shows played · # of emails sent

A few important notes: It's really hard to identify the goals that'll be *most* impactful in reaching your desire and the activities that'll be *most* impactful in helping you achieve your goals. (This is why it's so easy to cave into all of the noise out there and bounce around to different promotional tactics without ever sticking for long enough to see results — or to get overwhelmed and do nothing.)

But it's not that hard to identify goals and activities that will *probably* be impactful.

And taking action is better than not doing anything. Because it's easier to tell if something is working than it is to predict if something will work.

So, plan out what you think will probably work. And then, as you go, evaluate whether what you're doing actually is working. You'll generally find that 20% of your efforts are yielding 80% of your results toward your goals. When you find what works, double down.

And remember, none of this is set in stone. Somebody is probably publishing a new book or course as you read this. I hate TikTok, but maybe next year it'll be the best platform to be on. Things are changing. You are, too.

Don't be stagnant. This is an ongoing process. Here's what its upkeep should look like.

Reevaluate all of these pieces — your core values and your ideal community — each year. Take a day to step back and ask if you still want the same things. Ideally, go somewhere to do this — book a cabin or a room in another town, break out your favorite core value and community visualization exercises, and figure out if you still want the same things you said you did a year ago.

Check in on your goals during each release cycle. Note what you have accomplished, and whether or not your accomplishments aligned with your core values and ideal community. Then, plan out your goals for the next release cycle.

Analyze the effectiveness of your activity each month. Measure your results to see if they're helping you reach your goals. Each month, double down on what's working, and swap out things that aren't working with things that you think will.

Last thing before we move on — as you track progress toward your goals, make sure you're measuring leading indicators. These are the things that will positively impact the completion of your goal in the future, as opposed to telling you whether or not it's happened in the past.

To illustrate this: If your goal is to lose weight, a good leading indicator is your number of weekly workouts. Track that. You can control how many times you work out, and that number directly influences your desired outcome. Don't track the number of pounds lost as carefully. It's not a leading indicator. You can't directly control it; it only tells you whether you were successful. In general, you should measure things like number of workouts, not like number of pounds lost.

Leading indicators should give you a simple, single lever to impact an outcome.

Your 3-2-1 *Goal Plan*, as a whole, will give you a focused way to build your community effectively.

Get Feedback

This is the last stage of laying the framework before we're ready to talk promo platforms. This stage is an important one, because it'll shape how and where you promote your music.

Here's the gist: Get an objective perspective on your music before you promote it.

We can argue all day about whether objectivity is possible in music criticism (It is possible. Just saying.), but what's important here is the fact that there will be public perception of your music that you won't be able to personally anticipate. You might think you've made an Americana track, but the world might hear it as pop country. You might think your chorus is incredibly witty, but the vast majority of people might think it's dumber than Patrick Star.

You are not a good judge of how other people will perceive your music.

Since promotion is largely about getting other people to perceive your music, there's a gap here that needs to be bridged. This is why it's really helpful to get feedback on something before you promote it.

The big record labels do this all the time, and they collect far more data than you or I will ever hope to shake a stick at. It's how they know which tracks to push as singles — and even what their tracks should sound like in the first place. But the good news is that you don't need tons of data to get actionable insight. Remember, 20% of anything gets 80% of the results. You don't even need to poll 50 people. Poll 10 and you'll get a good idea of what you're working with.

You should have two goals in getting feedback.

First, you'll want to understand if your music is any good. We're not talking *objectively* good here; we're just considering whether or not people will probably like it enough to listen to, share, and cover it — if it's good enough to qualify as meaningful and to build a community. If people probably won't like your music enough to do those things, then you probably shouldn't spend time and effort promoting it. This is a tough reality, but it's important.

If the feedback you get shows that your music isn't good, please don't let it keep you from making more music. Take it as inspiration to stay consistent and to work on your capabilities. Remember that Bob Dylan wrote a lot of bad songs, too.

Second, you'll want to understand who will like your music. What genre will it fit in? What other artists does it remind people of? The answers here will help you to focus on promoting your music to the people who will actually like it.

There are plenty of ways to ask for feedback; sites like SubmitHub and Groover are meant to provide it, to some degree. But here's a simple and free approach that I recommend.

Don't pay for feedback to start. Use your friends, family, and random people in the grocery store if necessary. Ask ten people four questions:

    1. On a scale from 1 (definitely not) to 10 (definitely),

how likely would you be to listen to this music multiple times if you didn't know me?

2. On a scale from 1 (definitely not) to 10 (definitely), how likely would you be to recommend this music to a friend if you didn't know me?

3. What are three artists this music reminds you of?

4. What is one word you would use to describe this music?

Make it clear you're looking for honesty, not charity.

Obviously, your results will be shaped by your selection of 10 people. Try to get a decent representation of music professionals, music lovers, and people who know what music is. But even if your sample isn't perfectly representative of the population (it certainly won't be), it should give you enough data to shape your approach.

Add up all of the answers to questions one and two and take the average. If either answer is at an average of five or below, you might want to pause before you push into promo. At the very least, dig into why the results aren't great.

If you pass, use question three to make a list of the 30 artists and acts your music is being compared to. Choose what you think are the top 10 and add them to your *Artist Impact List*. If there's overlap and multiple people picked the same artists, great — go with that. If not, I trust you to make a decision that makes sense. You'll be using these references to shape your promo pitches and to guide where you pursue promotion.

Question four will be a helpful starting place as you write your EPK materials (which we'll cover in Chapter 14).

All right. We've laid the framework. You know what a community is and why it matters. You have some idea of what your perspective is and what you want your community to look like. You know what meaningful artistry takes: consistency, connections, and competency. You know what your goals are. And you know a little bit more about how your music will be perceived.

What we've covered so far is the core of promotion. If you stop here and don't read any further, but use this thinking to drive the selection and use of your tactics, you'll be well-positioned to succeed. Fill out the frame and your house will be solid.

For the rest of the book, I'm going to get much more tactical. But please keep in mind that good promotion doesn't start with tactics; what works on Facebook changes every day. Good promotion starts from a strategic understanding of what you're trying to accomplish.

The approach I'll be presenting shouldn't be taken as gospel. If you feel that a platform I suggest *won't* work for your community, or that a tactic I neglect to cover *will* — well, you might be right. I'm going to present what I've seen work, but please let your understanding of your own community, artistry, and goals inform your approach.

With all of that said: Are you ready?

Cool. Here we go.

SECTION II

The Tools

7

AN INTRODUCTION TO TOOLS

I n this section, I'll cover the underlying tools that should retain your audience whether or not you're releasing music — the platforms you'll set up and maintain on an ongoing basis. This section is about the setup. Start here; then in Section III, I'll lay out a strategy for promoting music as you release it.

To set the stage, I want to reiterate what the platforms and tactics I'll cover are for.

These things are designed to help indie artists promote their music, which means to build a strong community around their own meaningful music. They will also help artists to gain more fans and make money to create a sustainable career. They will help you to market *your* music: original music that you've created and that matters to you — and that's meaningful.

These tactics won't help you as much if you're creating covers of pop songs so that you can go viral. You won't see TikTok here. We're not going to be talking about brand sponsorships or making money as an influencer.

And, again, this isn't an exhaustive list of activities. I'm not documenting everything. I'm documenting the tools and platforms that I've seen work best for indie artists.

Let's dive in.

The Platforms

As of right now (we're talking worst-year-ever-2020), these are the things you should get set up before a release — or, in general, the things you should have running on an ongoing basis. I've roughly ordered them by level of priority.

1. Artist photos
2. Your website
3. Your email list
4. Spotify
5. YouTube
6. SoundCloud
7. Instagram
8. Facebook

If you don't have these things set up before you release music — and if you don't maintain them on an ongoing basis — you'll be at a disadvantage when you go to promote your music.

How to Think About Platforms

A few notes to help you frame things as we get started.

First, these are *promotional* platforms. There are other things you should set up, too, like your distribution platform (i.e.

DistroKid, CDBaby) and your membership with a performing rights organization (PRO). Logistical considerations like these are really important, but I don't consider them promotional tools as much as they are business tools. So, for direction on them, I'll point you again toward a music business book like Ari Herstand's *How to Make It in the New Music Business.*

Second, since this is a roadmap toward building community, I'm going to try to keep things focused in the direction you want to go. Obviously, there are limitless ways you can use YouTube or your website or Facebook. But I believe there are a few ways to use each channel that tend to work more effectively more often. So, in this section, I'll be focusing first on the *purpose* of each channel — what you, as an indie artist, should be using it *for.* This will shape *how* you'll use it. Then I'll list the essential elements you'll need on each channel to fulfill its purpose. (In the following section, we'll move from setup to release.) Finally, I'll list the most important metric to track on each.

Channel Purpose Cheat Sheet

Website

Purpose: To tell your story, grow your audience, and function as the hub for your promotion.

Metric to Track: Users per month

Email

Purpose: To drive your biggest fans to valuable actions.

Metric to Track: Conversion rate

Spotify

Purpose: To be the place fans listen to your music.

Metric to Track: Followers

SoundCloud

Purpose: To send industry people your music for easy streaming.

Metric to Track: N/A

YouTube

Purpose: To turn listeners into fans.

Metric to Track: Subscribers

Facebook

Purpose: To reach new fans, prove credibility, and encourage valuable actions.

Metric to Track: Followers

Instagram

Purpose: To reach new fans, tell your story, and encourage valuable actions.

Metric to Track: Followers

YOU SHOULD CREATE a sheet called a *Platform Scorecard* to track each of these important metrics over time. Note each one monthly. This will let you measure your growth.

In all of this, my hope is to keep you focused on what's most impactful toward your success.

Here's the mistake a lot of musicians make when they market their music: They treat these channels like toys instead of like tools.

Hey, I'm all about toys (not that I still have my collection of Mighty Beanz or anything). Toys are great because they don't have a defined purpose; they're just fun in themselves. But your channels should serve a purpose. Each channel, from Facebook to YouTube to SoundCloud to whatever, takes time to set up and maintain and use. That's time that you could be spending writing songs, doing shows, or playing with Mighty Beanz. So, be thoughtful. Don't waste your resources — don't cave to the pressure to be on everything. You shouldn't get a channel unless you know how you want to use it and what you want to use it to do. Yes, how you use it can shift over time, but if you don't have an idea going in, don't go in.

With that in mind, when you use a platform, you should ask which of the pillars of community it best supports, ask how you can use it to support those pillars, and then put it to use intentionally to do that.

I've found that the pillars of community roughly align to the stages in a marketing funnel.

You've probably heard of marketing funnels before, but here's the overview: Buyers (or fans) move through progressive stages toward more and more valuable actions. Graphically, this looks like an inverted pyramid; the decreasing size of each section is representative of the number of people who will enter into it. At the top of the funnel are people who've heard of you but have never engaged with your music. Then come the people who stream your music but never buy it. There are fewer people who've bought something — a shirt or an album. Even fewer people have bought multiple things and maybe been to a show. Only your hardcore fans buy every single thing you put out, like your mom and her friend Beth.

The funnel looks like this:

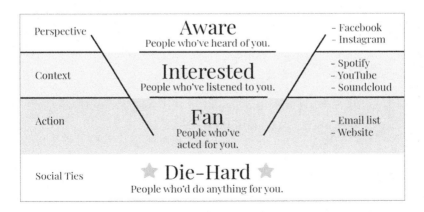

Again, each stage of the funnel can be roughly correlated to one of the pillars of community. And each platform should be focused toward one stage of the funnel.

Generally, the order of platforms listed above corresponds inversely to the stages in the funnel. Your base platforms — email list and website — are where you convert people into die-hard fans. This where the shared actions happen. Your music platforms are where you get people to listen. These serve as your community context. And your social channels are where you find people who might like you. This is where you define your perspective.

In reality, of course, this progression is not completely linear, the alignment of pillars to purpose isn't perfect, and platforms can also be used for multiple purposes. The world is gray, not black and white. A die-hard fan could buy all of your merch and stream your music on Spotify, but might ignore your exis-tence on Facebook. Shared actions can be encouraged on Face-book as well as through email. But, *generally*, this alignment is a helpful way of framing the purpose of things. It's a way of keeping in mind that these platforms are tools, not toys.

If you completely disregard any tactical advice I give but ask yourself "How will this channel build my community through shared perspective, context, or action?", then you'll do fine. If you use things haphazardly or inconsistently, you might get lucky, but you'll probably do terribly.

With this context in mind, let's dig into our promotional plat-forms. Here's what you should do for each.

8

BASE PLATFORM SETUP

These three pieces / platforms will be the base of your promotional efforts and the foundation of your community. All of your subsequent efforts will build on these. So, get them right. No pressure.

Artist Photos (and Art)

Art is technically not a platform, I know. Stop nitpicking. The purpose of your art should be to establish your image and build your credibility. Your art should build the community pillar of shared perspective and should begin to build shared context for your artistry.

Art is first up in our tactical discussion because it's the first thing people see when they engage with your music — whether in the form of a cover image or a band pic.

My advice (and this isn't mindblowing or the key to driving tons of fan engagement, but if you don't follow it, you'll end up driving fans away): Get good photos. Use good art. Look legit.

Look, I'm not a graphic artist or a photographer. But anyone can tell when a musician has taken their own photos on an iPhone 6 camera. Or when someone in the band's got a DSLR, a timer, and a brick wall to stand in front of. Or when someone has Photoshop and the ability to add the vignette effect. There are websites dedicated to making fun of bad band photos. You don't want to find yourself there. Worst of all, you don't want to sabotage your promo efforts by having people immediately tune out your music because the artwork is bad.

When I review music at *Two Story Melody*, if an artist has a bad photo, I'm ten times more likely to pass. There's just a high correlation between bad art and bad music. When I see a crappy iPhone pic, I'm biased before I even hit play.

So, what should you do?

Well, you should pay for a pro-level photoshoot. That's probably the best option. If you can afford to, do it. But let's be honest, you'd probably prefer not to spend too much cash on this — and I don't think you *have* to to get a result you can be proud of. You almost certainly have friends who are into photography, so hit them up and ask if they'd be willing to help you out by taking artsy pics of you. Be willing to pay them, too. They'll be way cheaper than some random pro, you'll have more fun, and, assuming they're half-decent, the outcome will get the job done. Two things, though: One, please have a vision, and two, don't stand in front of a brick wall.

What's a vision? Great question. A vision is the clear representation of your perspective into your art. There are two things your aesthetic vision must incorporate. First, it should represent your core values — likely in application to the topic you're covering. For instance, if a core value is encouragement and your song is about mental health, the vision of your art should communicate something encouraging about the topic — maybe a supportive community, or maybe a brightly colored illustration representing healing.

Second, your aesthetic vision should ideally align with people's perception of your music. Remember the feedback you gathered as you built your framework? Incorporate the words people used to describe your music into your artwork. If your friends called your music "honest", "raw", or "thoughtful", take photos that reflect those traits. Don't get all made-up or wear something business casual if people perceive your music to be "raw." Clarify and communicate your perspective. Follow the feedback, make it your own, and turn your art into a vision.

One tactical way to home in on your vision is to put your music into a physical place. When you wrote your songs, what physical place did you think of? What scene comes to mind when you listen to them? Even if it's not fully clarified, you've probably got some idea of where your songs take place. Develop that idea and use it in your art. Get photos in that place.

Consistent vision is the difference between art that's okay and art that's great. So, apply your theme across all of your materials. The 1975, for example, went with all black and white art for their self-titled album and then went with bright colors (and lots of pink) for their next. (Side note: I guess Matthew Healy pictures a weird industrial wall when he writes.)

On a very practical note, no matter what you choose, make sure you get photos of yourself in portrait and landscape orientations so you can fit profile pictures and cover photos for the various platforms. I've worked with a surprising number of bands that have one photo in landscape that gets cropped weirdly in coverage. Obviously, a professional photographer will help you to avoid this mistake, but if you're working with a friend, please make it a note to get images in a variety of formats.

Finally, you need the cover art for your music. My take on this: Unless you can get a top-tier pro to take your picture and design the art, or unless your music is heavily based on your image (like, you're very convinced that you're hot), don't use an image of yourself or your band as your cover art. And even if one of those scenarios applies to you, I'd probably opt for something else.

Because, if you're like most indie artists, nobody knows you (yet). Putting your face on the cover means nothing; it just makes you look a little full of yourself. Face-based cover art is for Taylor Swift and Ed Sheeran, because those are the types of artists people recognize. When I see Taylor Swift on an album cover, I think, "Oh, this is a Taylor Swift album." When I see some random person on an album cover, I think, "Oh, this person is trying to be like Taylor Swift."

Have the best graphic designer you're friends with make something that looks good. Something like:

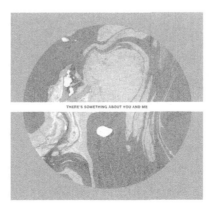

If you do decide to put your own face on the cover of your music, get a professional to take your photos.

Having good art with a consistent theme across all of your platforms will make you look ten times more legit — and this will make promoting your music ten times easier. Good art will be its own context, and it will allow your community to easily understand (and from there, share) your perspective.

Website

Your website should be the hub of all of your promo efforts. While its primary focus should be to incentivize shared actions, it can and should play a role in building perspective and context, too. It is your most important platform.

Most important? Yes, really. I know — with all of the platforms out there today, it can feel like the entire idea of a website is outdated. You've got enough places to build your audience, right? So many of them are practically built already; all that's left for you to do is sign up and create. Is it really worth it for you to put effort into creating a platform of your own?

It absolutely is, and here's why: Because a platform of your own lets you build an audience of your own that will be more engaged with your music.

Here's what I mean. If you built an audience on Facebook five years ago, they were your fans, sure, but they were really Facebook's audience; today, you basically have to pay to get your own fans to see your posts. If you build a huge following on TikTok today, great (I guess). You've got fans, but they're really TikTok's audience. Cross your fingers that the platform won't get sold or go under in two years, and while you're at it, pour one out for all of the Vine superstars who came before you.

When you build a website, though (and as we'll cover next, an email list), the platform's yours. And your chances of engaging with the people there are way better because those people are literally there for you – they're not scrolling through a feed where you happen to show up. I'm not saying social platforms aren't a great place to tell your story as an indie artist. They absolutely can be, and you should be there, too. All I'm saying is that having your own website is a necessity.

Okay. With that cleared up, let's get back to the point: What's the goal of your website?

Your website should serve three tactical goals. First, it should connect your story to your audience. In other words, it should be a place where your fans can learn more about who you are as an artist and engage with you and your music. Second, it should grow your audience — you should be tracking website visitors and collecting email addresses. Third, it should give your music context in the industry. It should be a place where promoters, labels, booking agents, press people, etc. can find out who you are and what you're about.

All three of these goals revolve around one premise: Your website should function as the hub of the wheel for your promo efforts. It's where everything gets connected. Theoretically, a person should be able to start at your website and trace out all of the spokes to find out all they could want to know about you as an artist. That means easy clicks through to your music, your merch, your Instagram, YouTube – whatever you've got.

It makes figuring out who you are a lot easier.

So, with those goals established, here's what you should include on your website to make them happen.

Legit photos. We've covered this, but here it is again. Good photos make a huge difference on a website. On your homepage, lead with your best landscape-oriented photo from your current or most recent project.

Your music. This is kind of a no-brainer, but yes, you should definitely have your music on your site. Of course, your site probably won't be the first place your fans go to listen to your stuff – once they know you, they're going to find you on Sound-Cloud or Spotify or Apple Music or whatever. But your site will often be the first place that new people (especially industry people) listen to your music, so you should make it easily accessible.

That means you should put up links to your streaming platform profiles, but also go ahead and embed your stuff so that people can hear it right there. If you want to take things as far as setting up streaming capability and hosting the tracks on your site, go for it (although nobody that I know likes when things auto-play, so maybe avoid that).

Less-important-but-still-cool: listing your lyrics. I trust artists' versions of their lyrics more than I trust Google. A link to Genius works, too, but accessing lyrics on-site is my preference when I'm covering an artist.

An email signup form. I'm huge into this, and we'll cover it in more detail in a bit. For now, just note that you should feature your email list signup prominently on your website. This should be the first or second thing people see. It shouldn't be buried in your footer.

A well-written bio. You can get someone else to write one or write your own, but when people find your website, they're going to want to read about you; on almost any site that lists it as an option in the main navigation, the About section is the second or third most-read page. People want to know what other people are about. That's the basis of pretty much any relationship, including artist-fan connections. This is an easy way to start communicating perspective and building context.

We'll cover how to write a bio in chapter 14.

Press coverage. People like press coverage for the same reason we like reviews of movies – we like to see what other people think about something while we're shaping our own opinions. Including press excerpts and links will serve the dual purpose of giving your fans more context into your story and giving industry people some positive reinforcement about how great you are. This is a step toward capitalizing on contagion theory (the idea that observing others acting incites action).

A blog. This one's not quite as necessary (your site could survive without it), but I think if you don't blog you're passing up on the potential to communicate your perspective and build context. Your blog can be a great platform to build a strong connection with your fans. I'm all about the blogs of some of my favorite artists – and, in some cases, they're my favorite artists because of their blogs.

Your merch. This is one of the most important functions of your site: selling your merch online. It used to be trickier from a technical perspective, but today there are a ton of easy platforms to sell from with minimal stress. Big Cartel is one solid option; Shopify is good, but expensive; Bandzoogle has merch setup built in. Regardless of the solution you choose, your site is the place your fans will go to buy your stuff. Fans dig merch. Make sure they can find it.

Your tour dates. Pretty simple. Ideally, your fans should be able to see where you're playing and when you're playing, and then be able to buy tickets (either directly on the site or through quick, accessible links). If they can, nice. If not, make it happen. Oh, and if you can help it, don't let your tour dates get outdated. It's very confusing.

Your socials. Last but not least, your site should definitely include easy links to your social channels. Again, it's the hub of the wheel for all of your efforts. List these in the header or footer.

The Facebook pixel. This is a snippet of code that will allow you to associate your website visitors with their Facebook profiles. It's the key to showing Facebook ads to your website visitors. To get your pixel, you'll need to have your artist Facebook page created. Once you do, go to Facebook's Event Manager, click "Connect Data Sources", and choose "Web". Select the Facebook pixel, hit "Connect", and name your pixel (use your website domain). From there, you'll be able to copy and paste the code into the header of your site. In WordPress, you can download a plugin to make this easy; on platforms like Squarespace or Bandzoogle, you'll find settings built in.

Google Analytics. This will be another snippet of code, and it will allow you to track your website traffic through Google's platform. You'll need to sign up for Google Analytics and create a property; from there, you'll create a basic reporting view. You'll get a tracking ID to add to your site — go ahead and add it in the same way you added Facebook's pixel. Now, you'll be able to start measuring how well your site performs.

And that's pretty much all that you'll need to get started.

But how do you actually build the site?

This is really a topic for another book, but I figure you deserve a quick primer on how to bring all of this into existence. For our purposes here, I'm going to assume you've never encountered the internet before. If you're an old hand at this, feel free to skip this section. If you're nodding along for appearance's sake but aren't really sure if you get it, no judgement — read on.

Here's what you'll need to have a website: a site (files and a database), a hosting provider (a computer server), and a domain name (a web address like twostorymelody.com).

To understand on a basic level how these three components work together, let's use the analogy of a car in a garage.

The car is your website. It's a physical thing, kind of — in this case, it's the collection of files sitting and a database sitting on a computer server somewhere. That computer server, or host, is the garage. You can move your car around to different garages; you can move your site and its files and database to different hosts and servers. Your domain name is the address of the garage. It's how you find the place where the car is being stored.

You need all three components to have a publicly accessible, working website.

Now, there are plenty of different ways to get all three of these things, and a lot of the time they come packaged together. GoDaddy, for instance, sells domain names starting at $0.99, and you can package these with hosting and site-building options at pretty affordable prices. There are plenty of other good ways to do this; I've built sites on WordPress, Squarespace, and Weebly, to name a few, and for the most part you can make something solid on any of these (or similar) platforms.

But here's my recommendation for indie artist websites: Bandzoogle. I used to be an affiliate with them. I'm not anymore, but I still think they're good. Here's why.

None of the other platforms are designed specifically for musicians. Using WordPress, for example, is like trying to build a LEGO Millennium Falcon using a huge, generic set of LEGOs; using Bandzoogle is like getting the Millennium

Falcon kit (which would be the best decision you'd make today).

Bandzoogle is made for music sites, which makes setting up all the things I mentioned above (tour dates, merch, music, email lists) a lot easier. You can also knock out all three of the elements you'll need (the site, the domain name, and hosting) through their tools. Plus, they've got phenomenal support and pretty affordable pricing.

So, there you go.

But no matter what you choose (and no matter what you choose to put on your site), intentionally use your site to support the pillars of your community. Tell your story on your site. If you work through the consequences of those things, your site will serve you well.

The one metric to track on your website: monthly users. In Google Analytics terms, a user is a person who visits your site. If one person visits your site eight times in a month, they'll only count as one user. I prefer this over page views and sessions because those metrics can be more easily impacted by behavioral outliers. If someone clicks through your website fifty times in a month, your page views and sessions will look better, but your fan count won't be significantly impacted.

Email List

Your email list should be the primary way you communicate to your core audience of fans. It will be one of your biggest means of inspiring your fans to the actions that are bigger than streaming — things like coming out to a show or buying your merch. It should build your community pillar of shared actions.

Email lists are awesome.

Marketers are fond of saying that email has the highest ROI of any channel (when compared to social platforms, search ads, paid spots — anything else, really). I've seen estimates that put email's return on investment as high as 40:1, which basically means that, if you spend $1, you make $40. That's insane. And probably, for indie artists, not entirely accurate. But still, when compared against ads on other platforms, it's certifiably nuts. Email is great for encouraging actions.

There are a few reasons for this. First, people check email a lot; the average person opens their inbox 15 times each day[1], which is more than people look at any social media platform. (The average Facebook user looks at the platform between two and five times a day[2], for comparison.) So, you're getting a lot of eyeball time. Second, email is a relatively low-cost channel. Mailchimp, for example, is free up to 2,000 subscribers, although past that it starts to get a bit pricey; at 2,500 subscribers, it's at least $49.99 per month. Benchmark is free for an unlimited amount of subscribers, but only allows you to send 250 emails a month. And Brian Hazard of Color Theory recommends Fanbridge, which is a little less sleek but is super efficient at $20 a month for up to 20,000 emails.

Anyway, the point is that, through email, you can potentially reach a ton of people without paying very much at all. It's a great bang for your buck.

And, while this isn't directly related to ROI, I want to point it out again: Email subscribers are yours. They are your community. Not Facebook's. Not Spotify's. Yours. That matters, because it gives you a level of stability that you can't replicate in any other digital channel. If Mailchimp goes under, you can pull your contacts to another provider. If Spotify ever changes — well, just hope that doesn't happen.

And, because email lists are yours, you can often use them effectively on multiple channels. We'll get into this later, but that means things like targeting fans on Instagram with specific ads, or creating lookalike audiences on Facebook to reach people who match your audience profile.

All of this is to say that the value's there for email. Now, how should you get set up with an email service?

There are three steps you'll need to follow:

1. Sign up for an email marketing platform.

My recommendation is to start with Mailchimp, because it's easy, it's free until you're over 2,000 contacts, and it has a cool little monkey logo.

2. Set up the platform.

There are a few things to consider here. First, I'd recommend getting an email address set up at your website's domain to tie into your email marketing account. (In other words, you should send from you.are.legit@yourwebsite.com instead of you.are.lame@gmail.com.) Having professional email set up will be helpful on its own down the line when you communicate with industry folks; for now, it'll add a layer of authority to your email marketing platform and make you more likely to get into inboxes. Emails that are sent from @gmail.com are more likely to end up in spam folders.

While some website platforms (like Bandzoogle) have their own email hosting options, I recommend using G Suite for this. Just sign up for Google business email and follow the directions; it only costs $6 per month for a single email address. You'll need DNS (domain name server — usually the place you bought your domain name) access to complete the setup, because you'll be updating MX records. If you're on Bandzoogle, they can help.

Back in your email marketing platform, you'll need to verify that you actually own the domain you'll be sending from. In other words, you can't send email from you.are.legit@yourwebsite.com if you don't own the domain yourwebsite.com. Different email marketing platforms will verify this in different ways (perhaps through an email or through adding a record to your DNS — the place you bought your domain name from). Just follow the directions the platform gives you.

Admittedly, these things can get a bit technical. Here's a word of advice: You can figure things out and you shouldn't pay someone to manage this stuff. Treat this as another skill to learn. If you get stuck setting things up, a quick Google search can almost always help you get unstuck.

3. Set up a signup form on your site.

I won't get into the technical aspects of doing this, because there are, as the (weirdly disturbing) saying goes, a million ways to skin this cat. But here's the strategic base you should consider:

Make signing up easy and put your form somewhere obvious. In other words, I recommend only requiring an email to sign up, instead of asking for full name and birthday and favorite ice cream flavor and whatever else. And don't bury your form in your footer. Put it in plain sight. Popups are annoying but they work. I'm generally a proponent of making your signup form the first or second thing people see when they view your homepage.

You should also create a single page on your site that's dedicated to getting email signups. This way, if you run campaigns to encourage signups, you'll have a single, simple place to send people. Mailchimp will give you a free landing page, but I recommend setting up a page on your own site, because you have more control over the look, feel, and information there.

Incentivize signups. Basically, give people a reason to join your list. One of the most common ways of doing this is to offer a free download of music in return — if it's unreleased, even better. You could offer behind-the-scenes updates on recording or tour dates. But please don't just say "Subscribe." Give them a reason to do it.

Automate this process. You should be able to set up your email marketing platform so that people who fill out the form are automatically added to your list and automatically receive access to their incentive. You absolutely don't want to be doing this manually. I'd also recommend setting up a welcome email that automatically thanks people for joining your list and lets them know what to expect now that they're on it.

Last word on that automation: If you feel comfortable with it, I'd recommend that, in your welcome email, you ask your subscribers to add your email address to their contact list. If a subscriber adds your address to their contact list, they'll see your emails in their inbox. If they don't, there's a decent chance that sometimes you'll go to a spam folder, or to the Promotions folder in GMail. Those places are bad. It kind of sucks to email people and have them not even see it.

We'll talk more in Section III about what emails to send as you release new music, but for now, a final and important tip on building your list: Track your conversion rate.

This is the ratio of signups against total website visitors (users). An average conversion rate is between one and two percent, which means that if 100 people visit your website, one or two will sign up for your email list. Tracking this number will allow you to test tactics to improve it. For example, you may find that adding a popup form is a really effective way to increase signups. Or you may find that changing your incentive for signup has a big impact.

The goal should be to get your conversion rate substantially above the two percent line. If you consistently get five or more signups per 100 visitors, you're doing really well. If you get 10 signups per 100, stop testing and let what's working keep working.

9

MUSIC PLATFORM SETUP

These three platforms (Spotify, SoundCloud, and YouTube) will be where fans and industry folks go to listen to your music. They will provide some of the primary contexts for your artistry. For now, we're not talking about how to push yourself on these platforms — we're talking about how to put yourself on them in a way that'll make you look good.

You should be able to set up each of these channels with little to no trouble. There are a few things to watch for on each, though (and a few tricks of the trade that'll make you look more legit).

Spotify

Your Spotify account's purpose is to be the primary place people listen to your music. It will heavily contribute to your community pillar of shared context.

I don't need to bore you with the stats, but I will anyway: Spotify is the biggest player in the streaming game, with 124 million paid subscribers to 60 million for Apple Music and 55 million for Amazon (last count in the final quarter of 2019[1]). That's a lot of people, and they listen a lot; the average Spotify user listens to 25 (ish) hours of music on the platform each month. Yes, you only get paid a paltry $0.004 (ish) per stream, but if you rack up a million streams (which is very feasible) then you've got $4,000. That's not a primary income stream, but it's not unhelpful, either.

You get it, I'm sure. Spotify is a place you should be, at least for now. Obviously, any major distributor will get you there.

Setting up your profile is pretty straightforward, but there's an important note: You do need to have music on Spotify *before* you can set up your Spotify for Artists account. Again, this is easily done through your distributor (I recommend CDBaby or DistroKid).

Once you do have music listed, go to artists.spotify.com to "claim your profile." Basically, this will give you access to edit your artist page content, plus the ability to submit future releases for consideration in editorial playlists (more on this later).

Here's how I recommend getting set up:

Art-wise, you'll need the basics. That means your profile image (a square that'll be cropped to a circle — and this *is* the time to use your face!) and your cover photo (grab your favorite landscape orientation shot from last chapter). Your profile image should be at least 300 x 300, but to make sure you get the best resolution across different devices, go bigger. Your cover photo should be at least 2660 x 1140. For this, make sure the object of focus is in the middle; doing that will keep the important things in view when the photo gets cropped differently on different devices.

I also recommend that you try to get a "Canvas". This is a looping video image (a .gif, basically, although they want it as an .mp4 file) that shows on listeners' screens when they listen to one of your songs on Spotify. As of mid 2020, this is in beta, and unless you're a VIP, you're not likely to get one — yet. But there's a waitlist you can sign up for, and you should do it. The best bet is that this will get rolled out to everyone within the next few years, and early metrics point toward it contributing to increases in shares and streams.

You'll also want your artist bio on hand; this will go in your "About" section. Again, we'll cover how to create your bio in Chapter 9. One note here, though: Make sure to include a link in your "About" section to your website.

While you're getting set up, I recommend that you create a playlist and make it your "Artist Pick". You'll have to do this from your Spotify user account, then select the playlist URL and paste it in on the Spotify artist side. This playlist will show in your profile and it's an easy way to continue building your context by engaging with fans and giving them another place to listen to your music.

There are two ways I'd recommend structuring this playlist. The first is to use it to bring fans into your creative process. If you take this approach, make your playlist something like "Songs that make me want to write songs" or "The [your current project] soundtrack". The other approach is to use this spot as a genre-placing promo opportunity. If you go for this, include your genre in your playlist name: "Dope Indie Grunge" or "All-time Americana". Go back to your documented feedback and use it here — add songs from the artists that your friends think are similar to you. If you choose to, you can promote this playlist, and if you get followers, you'll have an instant platform for your own music when you release it.

Note that these two methods of creating playlists aren't mutually exclusive; you could do both. But unless maintaining playlists is what you want to be spending time on, I'd recommend focusing on one approach so that you don't overburden yourself.

Finally, if you have merch (and you should), you should get set up to sell it on Spotify (if you can). To do this, you'll need to apply for membership at Merchbar. There's not much to the application process and it's free to apply, but you're not guaranteed to get in; they get hundreds of submissions a day and reject a lot of them. If you do get in, though, Merchbar will pull your items from whatever platform you use (Shopify, Tictail, BigCartel, etc.) and show them right on your artist page. Users who click will be sent to your shop.

The most important metric to track on Spotify is followers; this is most closely correlated to a show of your community's strength. Streams and monthly listener numbers are trendy — they look good but they don't represent long-term progress. You can get added to a big playlist and get a million streams and a ton of monthly listeners, but that doesn't mean you have a million fans. Followers matter more. They'll see your new music in their new music playlists (like Discover Weekly and Release Radar) and have you algorithmically added to plenty of their random-ish playlists (like Your Daily Drive and random Daily Mixes). They represent more lasting growth.

The good news and bad news is that you can't do a ton on your Spotify channel to drive followers. That's good because you don't have to spend time on this on the profile side. It's bad because you can't as easily impact it. People just have to click the button.

Got your artwork, bio, artist pick, canvas, and Merchbar set up? Tracking followers? Congratulations — your Spotify foundation has been laid. Now it's onto the next channel.

SoundCloud

SoundCloud's purpose will be to send industry people easy-to-stream links. It's a point of context.

As a result, here's the truth: You shouldn't pay too much attention to SoundCloud other than as a delivery method. It's sole purpose will be to act as an easy channel for sending people your music. It's important because it'll facilitate a lot of your other promotional efforts, but unless you're doing hip hop or EDM, use it for this purpose and don't stress past that. If you're doing hip hop or EDM, you may find SoundCloud useful as a promotional platform, but even so, I think there are better approaches to take. It's not incredibly important to develop an audience on the channel itself.

The reason I recommend SoundCloud as the basis for promo efforts is that, unlike Spotify (which is built to work primarily as a downloadable app and requires that listeners have an account to hear an entire song), SoundCloud makes streaming easy for absolutely anyone. All they've got to do is click a link to listen. This makes it the ideal platform for sending tracks when you're doing promo — better than Spotify, Dropbox, or an .mp3 (for sure).

Because your SoundCloud will function as a place for industry people to hear your music, you should set it up to cater to them. Here's what you'll need: your artwork, your bio, and links back to your website and social channels. That's it.

In terms of setup, the only note here is to keep all of this relevant. It's a bad look when you pitch a publication for coverage, then send them a link to a SoundCloud profile that clearly hasn't been updated in two years and includes a link to your early-high-school Bandcamp. Spend twenty minutes setting this up correctly. Then move on.

You don't need to track anything here. This platform is a means, not an end.

YouTube

You should use your YouTube channel as a place to build your image, catalogue your music, and showcase all of your video content. It's a great place for building shared context and communicating your perspective.

YouTube obviously has a ton of potential as an audience-building platform; 1.9 billion people log in each month.[2] There are good ways to reach these people, but I think that, unless you're primarily a YouTuber, the channel is best as a showcase piece — at least to start. Find people on other channels, and as they're checking your stuff out, use YouTube to make them fall in love with it (then you).

There's a lot to work through here. YouTube is about fifty times fancier than SoundCloud, and there are a lot of options that you can use (or disregard) to customize your channel. Here's what you should do.

As you begin, if you can, you should get an "Official Artist Channel" (or OAC for short if you want to be hip). There are a variety of benefits to this, including more advanced visibility into your analytics, easy categorizing of your music for ol' Google, and increased visibility in search. Getting an OAC is easier than getting some of the tools mentioned earlier on Spotify, but you do need to have an existing channel. All you need is control over that (meaning that it can't be a joint channel with other artists) and three previously released videos that are available on YouTube and were delivered through your distributor. To make your channel an OAC, you'll need to go through your distributor. DistroKid and CDBaby make this pretty easy. If you run into trouble, get help from your distributor's customer support. That's what they're there for.

Whether you can get an OAC yet or not, you'll want to get set up with the basics.

First step: the name. This should be your artist name, not something weird. Go for easy search value over cleverness. When people search for your music, your channel should come up.

Second step: the art. You'll need your banner image again (2560 x 1440) and a "channel icon" — make this your profile picture.

Third step: the videos. YouTube lets you feature a video in the "top shelf" — the area users will see first when they hit your channel. I'd recommend putting your current project here. The alternative is to make a channel trailer video, which is more trouble than it's worth if you're not a YouTuber.

If you get an OAC, YouTube will automatically sort your music into a discography. If you don't have an OAC yet, make a playlist — definitely of your own stuff, and maybe a separate playlist of some influence tracks, too.

Fourth step: all of the other stuff. Your bio should go under your "About" section. You should include links to your other platforms on top of your banner image. Make the other spokes of your wheel easy to find. And again, keep your information up to date and your vision consistent.

To that end, if you haven't yet, you should also add custom thumbnails to your videos. Thumbnails are the screens that show when videos are suggested or embedded — the still shots before people click. Customizing them takes a bit of time, but I recommend doing it because it gives your channel an added level of credibility, keeps your aesthetic consistent, and increases click-through rate (by up to 100%) on your videos when they show up as suggestions in other places. Note that you'll have to verify your channel in order to do this — that can be done through Settings.

Finally, at this stage, the most important metric to track and build on your channel is your number of subscribers. You can push video views during release campaigns, but, during setup, put the mechanisms in place that will encourage subscriptions. YouTube does some of this automatically. For instance, they'll usually put a "Subscribe" button next to your video description in most viewing formats. But the most impactful way to improve subscription rate is to add clickable links from your video.

There are two potential ways to do this. The first is to have a clickable "watermark" (an image that hovers in a lower corner of your video and can be clicked through). Make this image a button to subscribe and link it accordingly. The second is to add a subscribe "card" that appears at the end of your video.

You can set both of these things up in YouTube's Creator Studio. I recommend doing both, because most people won't watch your video all the way through (so having a mid-view action is nice), but the end of the video is the most effective spot to encourage action (if people get there).

10

SOCIAL PLATFORM SETUP

These two channels suck.

I'm only kind of kidding. On a personal level, I'm so tired of Facebook and Instagram. I've wasted way too many hours scrolling through pictures of things I don't care about. I've seen way too many obnoxious political posts that make me want to crush a soda can. I've rewritten way too many words to try to find the perfect level of irony for my Insta captions (don't worry, I always get it right, but it takes an hour and a half).

But, also, I'm so grateful for some of the real connections I've made in meaningful communities online.

My most recent personal project (*Indiana* — you can find it on Spotify if you search for "Jon Henry") was a collection of songs and stories written about my grandparents wrestling with my grandmother's dementia. We named the project after their hometown, Indiana, Pennsylvania, because we felt like the place represented, in a physical way, a lot of what we wanted to say. The town is fading and changing; so were my grandparents. There's a college that dominates the local culture in a way that it didn't two decades ago. Main Street looks different. A lot of people have left. A lot of older people still live there.

Anyway, my dad (who grew up there) is part of a Facebook group called "You know you're from indiana pa if..." It's this collection of people who are from the place, and a lot of the interactions in the group center on memories. "Remember when Anderson's shoe store was here on this street?" Or, "Anyone seen this photo of Jimmy Stewart (Indiana's favorite son) with a friend fishing at Blue Spruce?" Or, "Here's the street I lived on when I was growing up!"

When we released our EP, my dad posted the songs from it into this Facebook group. And immediately, all of these people I've never met were messaging me and signing up for my email list and buying the album and saying how impacted they were. I had middle-aged men telling me how the music reflected their memories of their childhood homes. Sweet old ladies were telling me they were listening to the songs in their homes alone and crying and remembering their kids. And it was all because of some random Facebook community my dad belonged to.

Here's my point (and no, it's not that my target audience may be 76-year-old western Pennsylvanian women, which is actually awesome): Social media can suck, but if it's used in the right ways it can also be incredibly fulfilling. It can literally change people's lives. It can get your music in front of the people who will most resonate with it. It can even create a community where one didn't exist before.

So, use it well.

Again, these channels are tools. Facebook and Instagram can help you to find people who will listen — to identify the people who will share your perspective and then deliver your perspective to them. In my view, they're the two channels that coincide most closely to top-of-funnel activity. The purpose of both should be to grow your audience.

Here's how to set them up.

Facebook

Facebook's purpose should be to reach new fans, demonstrate your credibility, and encourage valuable actions.

Look, I know that Facebook's kind of old hat by now. It's 2020. We have about eight different social media platforms that are each about eight times as cool as the ol' book. It's been dragged through the mud for featuring fake news and proliferating middle-aged comment wars about politics. All valid points, I'll admit — but still, everyone and their aunt is on Facebook. There are over 2.5 billion monthly active users. And it's also the engine that drives Instagram advertising. So, if you're serious about marketing your music, Facebook, although it's old hat, is still a hat you've got to wear.

Here's how to set it up.

First of all, you'll need an artist page. If you've spent any time on Facebook (hopefully you've spent some but not too much), you'll know that this is separate from your personal Facebook account. This page is what will allow you to run ads. Facebook has a few different types of pages you can create; go with "Community or Public Figure" and then choose the category "Musician / Band." As is hopefully obvious, this will get you going with the page settings that are most applicable to musicians and bands.

The setup work on Facebook is pretty similar to what you've done on other platforms. Title your page your artist name. If your artist name isn't available, use easy variants (like adding "music" to the end of your name). Set up your profile picture and cover photo using your go-to artwork. There are options to add videos and other fancy things, but there's no need to do this unless you've got something that fits already, because the benefits of fanciness don't outweigh the time it takes to create these pieces. Fill in your Story section with your bio. Include links back to your website and other platforms. Keep things up to date. You know the drill by now — stay smart and you'll be off to a good start.

That said, there are two things I recommend setting up on Facebook that are unique to the platform. The first is to use your page's Button to link to your email list. Keep in mind that the deeper into your funnel you can bring people, the better, and while Facebook can (and should) be used to incentivize actions, its primary role should be to help people enter into your world by clarifying your perspective. Remember the email landing page you set up on your website — the one built specifically to encourage signups? Create a button with the call-to-action to "Sign Up" and set it to link to that page.

The second thing I recommend is buying 1,000 page likes. Don't panic. I haven't gone insane (as far as I can tell). I don't mean that you should pay for likes from one of those sketchy sites that uses stock art from the early 2000s and promises "REAL (NOT FAKE!!!) FOLLOWERS!". That would be bad — like, bad enough that Facebook will get on your case about it and maybe shut down your page. So, please, do not do that.

What I do recommend is taking advantage of Facebook's own advertising platform to run campaigns at the lowest possible cost to boost your follower and like counts.

Admittedly, this technique can feel uncomfortably close to a used-car sales tactic. Read through the approach, and if you don't want to spend time doing this, skip it. My opinion is that it can be helpful toward the worthwhile goal of building a strong community, but it's only a fire starter; there are other ways to get the blaze going, and if you'd prefer to use matches and kindling instead of artificial lighter fluid, I understand your thinking.

Before we move into the tactics of the approach, I want to make two notes. The first is that this section (and, by extension, this book) is not meant to be an in-depth guide to running social ad campaigns. Really, books aren't a great media for this, because digital platforms change too quickly. Ad platforms have their buttons and settings updated every other week. The good news is that there are plenty of great resources available to build basic ad skills. If you are serious about social advertising, take advantage of these great resources by investing in a basic primer course on social media ads for artists. My top two recommendations to build this skill are Indiepreneur courses (which are very affordable at $37 for monthly access — you can join and cancel when you've completed the course) or Omari's Facebook and IG Ads for Musicians (which you can access for free if you work with the company on a promo campaign).

Remember: In advertising (as in most things), what's most important is the thinking behind the tactics. If you know the rationale (what you're trying to accomplish and why), it's easier to figure out the how (what buttons to click), even as the tools change.

The second note is that it's increasingly feasible to automate your social campaigns with third party platforms. Basically, you can pay a small additional fee on top of your ad costs and get ready-made campaigns running quickly that actually work very effectively. I'll cover this in more depth in Chapter 15; actually, I think that using third-party services for ads makes sense, because it saves a ton of the time and money you'll inevitably lose through trial-and-error. My recommendation on promo in general is to test things yourself when testing doesn't involve spending money, and to pay for proven results when testing does require spending money.

That said, I also believe that it's helpful to have a baseline understanding of the promotional activity you're going to invest in. It makes more sense to buy a good guitar when you know a little bit about guitars; it's easier to pay for good promo when you know a little bit about promotion.

So, here's what you should do: Run a low-budget campaign to familiarize yourself with how social ads work.

To get set up on Facebook, I recommend running a "Page Like" campaign targeted at relevant geographic locations and demographics.

First, let's walk through the rationale, and then I'll walk through the methodology. Why should you pay for page likes? What good do they do?

The good they do is to build your credibility through social proof — and this is a big benefit. This, again, is contagion theory in action. If you have less than 1,000 page likes, you absolutely look like a hobbyist. If you look like a hobbyist, many industry gatekeepers will, unfortunately, dismiss you out of hand.

Let's say you email your favorite music blog and ask for coverage of your upcoming release. If they engage with your email (a big if), they'll click through to your various profiles to take stock of what you're like as an artist. If, as they click through, they see that you only have 500 Instagram followers, only one song with over 1,000 plays on your Spotify profile, and only 600 Facebook likes, they'll assume you're doing this from your parents' basement — and they'll move on to bigger things. If, though, they click through your profiles and see one platform where you have demonstrated social proof (in the form of, say, 5,600 followers on Facebook), they'll listen to you to make sure they're not missing something, and from there they're far more likely to cover you. In this way, the perception of community can help you build a real one.

Now, you can absolutely build social proof on other platforms. I believe that Facebook is the best place to start building, though, for three reasons. First of all, there's a perception on some platforms that artists' audiences are based on appeals other than musical talent. People follow YouTubers, for example, because they're funny. People follow Instagram influencers because they're hot. But people follow bands on Facebook because they like their music.

Second, likes on Facebook tend to stand on their own as a metric. Whereas on Spotify, industry people will look for followers to be corroborated by corresponding metrics like streams and monthly listeners, or on YouTube they'll look for views in addition to subscribers, Facebook page likes speak for themselves. In other words, if you have likes on Facebook, people tend to assume that other people like your music. It's a great place to "seed your guitar case".

Third (and most importantly), it's simply easier and cheaper to grow page likes on Facebook than it is to grow similar metrics on most other platforms. The action is direct. Facebook makes it easy. And you can get very low costs per click.

So, as you're setting up Facebook, make it the first platform where you seek to demonstrate social proof.

Note, though, that the strategy I'm presenting here is *only* valuable as a social proof. When street performers seed their guitar cases to get started, they're obviously not making any money. In the same way, most of the page likes you'll get using this method won't translate into people who will take action to support your music (although some will).

That's the rationale. Again, if this doesn't align with your perspective, skip it.

If you go forward, you'll need to make a foray into the strange world of Facebook ads. Facebook's advertising platform is insanely powerful. I also happen to think it's annoyingly counterintuitive and poorly designed, but I guess you can't have it all. The important thing to start is that you navigate your way to the Ad Manager and don't try to run things from the Ads section of your page, where you have access to fewer, less-nuanced controls. Do this on a desktop. Click the down-arrow in the top-right corner and select the option to manage ads, then select your page, or just go to business.facebook.com and click to manage ads from there.

There are four major components to consider in any ad campaign. These are:

- The goal. This is the desired outcome or action that

you'll be seeking from your ads. In Facebook's Ad Manager, you'll define this at the Campaign level.

- The audience. This is the carefully defined segment of people you will be showing ads to. In Facebook, you'll define this at the Ad Sets level.
- The content. This includes ad copy and collateral like videos and images. You'll define this at the Ads level.
- The budget. This refers to the amount of money you'll spend on your ads over a specified amount of time. You can define this at a Campaign or Ad Set level.

We've already specified your goal: to get 1,000 page likes at a low cost. In Facebook's terms, we'll be running an Engagement campaign to get Page Likes. Specifying this option in the Ad Manager will allow you to create ads that have a very simple call-to-action: a button that users will click to like your artist page.

Your audience should be people who will be interested in your music and who live in your country and blue-chip locations like Europe, Japan, Australia, Canada, Hong Kong, and Brazil (you can certainly broaden this, but doing so is more likely to result in bot clicks). Make sure to select your own language as an audience requirement.

The next step in defining your audience will be to target users who are interested in music that's similar to yours. Facebook allows you to target the fans of large-scale acts. Using your list of similar artists from your *Artist Impact List*, pull at least three that you think will have fan overlap, making sure that you're able to target their fans in the Interests section of audience targeting — do this by searching for the artist page in the search bar. Include each one in your audience so that anyone who is a fan of any of the acts will potentially see your ad.

You should also narrow down your audience's age range to folks who will be most likely to engage with your genre.

Altogether, your audience size should be between 1M and 100M. If you need to combine multiple artists in the "Include" section of audience targeting, you can do so.

For your ads themselves, keep things simple. Write two sentences of copy. In the first sentence, identify the best way to label your music that will resonate with potential followers, and consider name-dropping the artist whose fans you'll be targeting. In the second, outline what people who follow your page can expect to see. For example: "Like Bob-Dylan-esque songwriting? Follow Leif Vollebek's page to see passionate, acoustic-driven live music and stay updated on new songs."

For the ad media, use your artist profile or cover image. You can also experiment with photos of live performances — just make sure that you're the focus of the shot, and that when the ad gets cropped, things still make sense. Altogether, try three or four different ad variations with different copy and images.

For budget, again, start small with an amount that you're comfortable with and can afford to lose. The good news is that, using this approach, page likes should cost you somewhere in the vicinity of a few cents each. So, $30 is a good start. But if you're looking at the last $30 in your bank account and debating whether to spend it on a Facebook ads campaign or dinner, please get dinner.

Set the budget to $5 per day, and set your ads live. Check back each day to see your results.

Don't use this method to gain more than 10,000 page likes; at that point, I'd consider your guitar case seeded. Remember, this approach is a means toward a strong community. It's not a strong community in itself.

One last note on this tactic: Continually improving your ad campaigns is a huge part of making them work well. You should experiment with changing each component of your ads — the image, the copy, and, most importantly, the targeting. When something works, do more of it. When something doesn't, pause the ad, or change it, and try something else.

Finally, your one metric to track on Facebook should be followers. These are different from page likes; people can like a page and not follow it for updates. If someone follows your page, they have a chance to see your posts. While Facebook's algorithm won't show your regular posts to most of your followers, this is still the metric that's most closely correlated to community strength.

Instagram

Instagram is an envy engine. I can't scroll through my feed without feeling like other people's lives are better than my own — that I'm unexciting and somehow missing out on something. When you use Instagram as an artist, your purpose should be to make *other* people feel that way.

Just kidding. Instagram, like most platforms, is not inherently evil. It can be awesome when it's used well. Its purpose should be similar to Facebook's: Use it to reach new fans, build context as an artist, and share your perspective. It's a top-of-funnel tool, but it has potential to serve nearly any community-building purpose.

Instagram used to be pretty simple to set up, but it's going the way of Facebook (which is to be expected, since it's owned by Facebook) and is becoming increasingly complex. Here's what you should do.

First, set up your profile to be a business account. This will allow you to do a few things (including, importantly, run ads) that personal profiles aren't able to do. You'll have the option to select either "Business" or "Creator". Make the obvious decision here, and then, for your subcategory, select "Musician" or "Musician/Band". These distinctions aren't hugely important, but they do play a role in how your posts get processed and eventually displayed by Instagram's algorithm, and you can also choose to have your category label displayed on your profile.

Next, if you're new, get familiar with the platform's behavioral norms and vibe. (If you're not new, take a moment to analyze and define the vibe you've experienced.) Out of the platforms I recommend for artists, Instagram is the one where it's most important to identify the existing culture, because it's the place you'll be acting most like a person (as opposed to acting like an act).

To do this, revisit the ten artists you want to emulate and, if you haven't yet, follow each of them on the platform so that you regularly see their posts. Get a feel for how they're doing things. Look at what they're posting, how they're structuring their captions, and what they're doing with their profiles. Note how their fans are interacting with them. Incorporate what you see as the best approaches into your own profile.

As you review the platform's culture, keep in mind that, in general, Instagram trends younger than Facebook; the average age of an Instagram user is under 34[1], while the average age of a Facebook user is over 40. That difference plays out in the normative behaviors for the two platforms. Millennial and Gen Z cultures set the standards on Instagram, which means that irony plays well, but so do authenticity and vulnerability — all of which are traits that tend to be less commonly displayed on Facebook. Your community, of course, will have its own subculture.

Once you understand the vibe, you have to create some context.

First, set your photos in the appropriate places. You can use your best artist photo for your profile picture, but if you want to use a photo that's more personal — like, an iPhone selfie or some piece of art that'd be relevant to your community — this is the place to do it. A lot of artists use Instagram as a kind of "backstage" platform. Less-polished content can let you communicate your perspective in a more direct, authentic way.

To start, the most important piece of real estate on your profile will be your bio. I recommend that you include two pieces of information: a line that clarifies your perspective as an artist, and a line about your current or most recent project. The first line, really, can be anything. You can take a straightforward approach and define your genre ("Folk music for pop people"), or you can make it a joke ("the artist currently known as phoebe bridgers"). The point is to provide some kind of hint toward what you stand for to give the first taste of your perspective. As with everything you do, this should flow from your documented framework.

The second line should give an update on your current project: "Touring the west coast rn. Get tix below." or "New EP out now."

On a business account, you'll get to input a website link that will show right below your bio. This link should always lead people to a page with an action step that will bring people more deeply into your community, and driving people to it will be one of the biggest purposes of your account.

A lot of Instagrammers use linktree (or something similar) to create the link here. Services like linktree create a simple page where artists can add all of their most relevant links to appear as buttons for quick access. This is a decent option, but my recommendation is to create a page that does this on your own website. You can add the same links, plus you'll get the ability to customize things a bit more — and, importantly, you'll be able to include an email signup form right on the page. Using this approach, Instagram can be an effective way to build your email list.

Next, on a business Instagram account, you'll get to define contact options. Include your official email account; it gives industry people an easy avenue for contact.

Finally, you'll need to post consistently to get value out of this platform. I don't consider social media setup complete until you've posted.

As you may have noticed, I didn't lay out a posting strategy for Facebook. That's because I recommend focusing the energy you put toward post generation on Instagram. Trying to maintain multiple channels is distracting; don't spread yourself too thin. Facebook posts reach fewer people, and you can easily translate your Instagram posts to Facebook (Instagram even gives you the option to do this automatically), so use Instagram as your primary post engine and you'll have fuel for both platforms.

Now, to tactics. There is not a magic posting frequency that will drive engagement rates, but like anything else, your Instagram profile will benefit from consistency. Studies have shown that posting once per day maximizes the reach of individual posts (meaning that more people see the photo in their feeds). Don't factor this data too heavily into your posting strategy, though, because Instagram's algorithm is always changing. Post at a frequency that feels sustainable to you and fits into the culture you've observed from your fans and the artists you're following. I recommend posting once per week, to start (although, if you want to prioritize Instagram as an engagement channel, you should post more often). If you can't commit to posting at least once per month, you should reconsider using the platform.

Remember, this is a tool. To use it strategically, I find that it's helpful to develop a *Posting Playbook* — a document that defines a few types of posts you can turn to when you're struggling to generate content.

Here are a few examples of post types you might include in your playbook:

Song background posts. Post a photo related to a song (the place the song was written or a lyric sheet, for example) and use it as a springboard to storytelling. In your caption, elaborate on the meaning behind the song.

Rehearsal / practice posts. Take photos or videos of band rehearsal and post them. In the captions, talk about the songs you're working on or make jokes about what's going on in the content.

Covers. Sit in front of a camera, cover a song, and post it. Tag the artist you're covering. It doesn't get more classic than this.

Gear stories. I love photos of guitars. Post your gear and tell the story behind it.

Daily routines. Showcase pictures of a daily routine — breakfast, or walks, or a snack, or (God forbid) a workout. These can feel self-indulgent quickly, but they can also draw your audience deeper into your perspective and context.

Tour diary. Post a similar photo for each venue you play on tour — showcase the front of each venue or the crowd. Tell a story from the day in each caption.

Content consumption. Post what you're reading, watching, or listening to. Tag the creator if they're on Instagram. Give your take on the art in the caption.

Sneak peeks. Post a sneak peek (video or photo) of the project you're currently working on. Use the caption to communicate details about the project.

Selfies. Again, this can feel self-indulgent, but studies show that selfies get higher rates of engagement, especially compared against posts that don't have people in them. Use the caption to go deeper.

Pets. Yes, pets. Of course. They don't even have to be yours.

Having a few types of posts defined will help you to stay consistent, because you'll minimize the barrier of idea generation — when you want to post something, you'll have options at the ready. In general, no matter what approach you take, produce content that defines your perspective and do your best to build context. Long captions are worthwhile.

I have three last notes on Instagram posting and tactics to conclude. First, use hashtags. Hashtags let you tap into existing conversations; your posts will potentially show when users search for tags you include, and you may even get organically displayed in the search tab to users Instagram thinks will like your content. In your *Posting Playbook*, pick 10 hashtags that are relevant to your perspective and tag them when your posts are relevant. This will broaden your reach.

Second, the best way to grow your reach (outside of paid ads) is through collaboration. Identify accounts that align with your perspective and your community and reach out to see if there are opportunities to interact. There are limitless ways to do this. You could cover each other's songs and tag each other, run joint contests, or release material together. The key, though, is to be an active participant in Instagram's community. Collaboration isn't just the key to expanding your audience — it's shared action as part of a community, which is the most fulfilling part of being on social media.

Third, keep up with the platform, but only in a way that aligns with your perspective. Like all platforms, Instagram is constantly adding new features and updating existing ones. Shopping functionality is coming, which will give your profile another way to encourage action. Other updates are sure to follow. I haven't specifically detailed how to use every option — like Instagram Stories or live streams or Instagram TV, for example — because I don't think these are *necessary* components to building community on Instagram at first, although they can certainly be incredibly helpful and do have their place (which I'll discuss in Section III).

This is important to remember: It's okay if you aren't on the cutting edge of everything. What matters most is that you're using the platform in a way that aligns with your perspective, goals, and community. You can easily slip into viewing Instagram as an end in itself. It's not. It's a means toward community around your artistry. Don't elevate it past that. Review the artists you follow and incorporate their best practices into your strategy, but don't feel obligated to do everything that everyone is doing. You will explode if you try to.

The metric to track on Instagram doesn't require much explanation: It's your number of followers. This is a highly visible measure of your community's size, and, while it's a bit of a vanity metric, it's helpful in building credibility and in enabling you to capitalize on contagion theory. Additionally, when you get to 10,000 followers, you'll be able to include links in your stories, which is a hugely effective way to share your art (and anything else). If you post good content regularly, use relevant hashtags, and collaborate with a like-minded community of creators, you'll be able to hit this within a year without using ads.

11

PLATFORM SETUP SUMMARY

I f you've made it this far, congratulations. Let's take a moment to note where you are and look back at what you've done in setting up your promotional platforms.

You've successfully set up all eight of the major pieces or platforms that will allow you to promote your music effectively.

Your artist photos represent your perspective, look legit, and are formatted to shine on each of the seven platforms you're using.

Your website reflects your perspective, is effectively building your email list with a conversion rate of five percent or more, and is functioning as the hub of the wheel for your promotional efforts.

Your email list is growing. You have a prominent opt-in on your website, you're linking to an email signup landing page from every social platform, and you're automatically rewarding your new subscribers with an incentive as they're added to your list.

You've ensured your Spotify account represents your perspective. If possible, you've made merch available from the platform. You've created an artist playlist that you'll use to build context or reach new listeners.

Your music is on SoundCloud and your information there is up to date. You don't care about SoundCloud.

You've registered an Official Artist Channel on YouTube, if possible. Your channel reflects your perspective and is optimized with on-video watermarks and buttons that encourage subscriber growth.

Your Facebook page represents your artistry and demonstrates your credibility with at least 1,000 followers.

You're posting on Instagram at least once a month (and ideally more often). You're collaborating with like-minded artists, using hashtags to tap into existing conversations, and focusing on the pillars of your community, not on noise.

Nice work. As always, remember: All of this is in service to a meaningful community built around your artistry. If any of these platforms or activities don't support that end, drop them. If platforms or activities not on this list would better support that end, add them. Just don't add TikTok.

All right. Your framework is documented. Your platforms are set up. Now, you're ready to put some music out.

Here's the roadmap to follow.

SECTION III

The Roadmap

THE STRANGE TRAIL OF PROMOTION

As we enter the final section of this book, we'll be covering what many people consider to be the meat of promotion: release strategies. In the pages ahead, I'm going to lay out a series of tactics that I've found to be helpful in promoting meaningful music, organized chronologically into three phases: first, what to do during the creative process, second, what to do in preparation for release, and, third, what to do when the music is out.

Altogether, this will give you a simple approach to reach more people and connect with them more effectively.

Because this information is by necessity so tactically focused, it can be a challenge to remember the guiding star that your promotional activity should follow: the intentional construction of community. To keep us aligned to that star — and to keep us from getting lost as we work heads-down through the weeds — I want to begin by examining the unorthodox example of someone who's walked the path before: indie savant Ben Schneider.

Schneider's promotional trails have been a bit strange.

In 2010, he was a dissatisfied graphic artist toiling for a marketing firm in Los Angeles who spent his working hours creating campaigns for poker companies and his free time working on an array of unconventional personal side projects.

These were not standard side hustles. They were legitimately weird. One of the most notable was a fake history exhibit for a fabricated scholarly society that promoted the idea that an ancient civilization had existed in Antarctica.

"People got [to the exhibit]," noted Schneider, "and they were just kind of confused."[1]

They could hardly be blamed.

Schneider is, as you might suspect, a bit eccentric. His art has benefitted from it. He got his first bit of momentum from distributing, not just CDs, but accompanying artwork, too, at a merchandise table at the Woodsist festival in Big Sur, California. His strength is that he doesn't just create music; he immerses music, as he described to *Vice*, in a created world:

> "It's just about telling as rich a story as possible. We use a variety of media to explore different facets of the story and the world of the album. Hopefully the end result is something more immersive, fun and meaningful."[2]

It's a unique approach to songwriting, and it's a big reason why, four years after quitting his marketing gig, Schneider was playing Lollapalooza with his childhood friends as the leader of a band most audience members couldn't name a single member of.

He created Lord Huron to be an experience.

Unsurprisingly, given his approach, the band has built an incredible context for its artistry. As *The New York Times* put it in the headline of a 2014 profile piece, the act is part musical project and part alternate reality game. The game part of that equation has seemingly escalated with each album release.

2015's *Strange Trails*, for instance — the band's second full-length album — was released along with a series of comic books and music videos that, together, compose a semi-cohesive narrative about the album's characters, many of whom belong to a fictional gang called the World Enders. The songs are based on a series of books written by Western novelist George Ranger Johnson, who, according to his website, was born in 1946 and lives in Tucson, Arizona — except that he doesn't actually exist. Reddit users proudly confess to spending countless hours following each thread of the story across every medium.

Vide Noir, the band's 2018 album, required even more commitment to unpack. It was prefaced by the group releasing seven songs to the world — or, more exactly, to seven geo-locations in the world. Listeners had to visit the album's website to get coordinates to the places (which included national parks, beaches, and a volcano), and in each of the spots, they were able to stream one of the seven songs.

It's a model of distribution that probably won't be coming to Distrokid anytime soon.

There is, clearly, copious planning that goes into each release, and worlds to unpack within each work. But here's the question that, for the purposes of this book, I'm most concerned with:

Is what Lord Huron does promotion?

Lord Huron's methods are counter-intuitive in that they don't directly boost play counts. Releasing a single that can only be heard at a volcano seems to burn any shot the band might have at generating impressive streaming numbers. And yet, given our definition of promotion, it's easy to see why the approach works. Remember: Promotion is not the practice of getting more plays; it's the practice of building a strong community around meaningful artistry. Those objectives, as we've seen, aren't always the same.

Like Billie Eilish's intentional dampening of "Ocean Eyes" to mainstream radio, Lord Huron's release strategies aren't designed to drive streaming numbers — but they are expertly crafted to encourage community action.

In fact, Lord Huron, intentionally or not, is quite good at building each pillar of community. They have a strong (if intentionally difficult to unravel) perspective. They've created (unreasonably) deep context. And, as we've seen, they encourage (sometimes quite costly) shared actions. The fanbase that travels to a volcano together stays together.

As a consequence, whether or not they'd consider their release models to be promotional, there's no doubt that they've built a community around meaningful artistry.

There's also no doubt that the approach has paid off. Lord Huron has headlined festivals, charted on Billboard's Hot 200, and been included on Barack Obama's 2018 list of favorite music. They will never be quite inside the mainstream. But they've found their people, and they will be able to make music for as long as Ben Schneider cares to keep making worlds.

As we dive into the dirt of tactics, it's helpful to keep Ben Schneider's example in mind. Successful promotion takes planning, but the guiding star of your release plan should be the purpose of community, not the promise of play counts.

While I'll present an approach that's straightforward, you should follow it only as far as it takes you toward your community, and you should be ready to chase your own star in unexpected directions. Because the bottom line is this: You can find your people, and you can do it as you create art that matters to you.

You don't have to walk the same strange trails as Lord Huron. But you will benefit, as their journey shows, from carefully building the pillars of your own community with each release you put out into the world.

In this final section, I'll walk you down a roadmap to follow.

As we begin, I'd like to provide some structure to your path. This final section is divided into three subsections: promotion during music creation, promotion to prepare for music release, and promotion for the release. It'll be helpful to frame all of this properly within the bigger picture of your artistry.

To build your community, this entire cycle should be a continuous process.

As I wrote when talking about consistency, you can't release an album every few years and expect your community to grow through the gap in your activity. If you're serious about being an artist, you should always be working on music, releasing music, or promoting music that's out.

Here's a framework I've found works well.

- Spend three months recording 10 to 12 songs.

- Over the next five or six months, release five or six of the songs as a series of singles.
- Release the full album after the singles.
- Over the next three months, release updated versions of the songs – acoustic takes, music videos, or remixes.
- Repeat the process.

As always, this is not the only possible framework, but it's helpful as a blueprint. Breaking things up this way will allow you to have a constant output of new material, and it will keep your audience engaged while allowing you to accumulate context. You'll always be working through a song cycle.

Before each cycle begins, you should revisit your *Core Values List,* your *Community Visualization Plan,* your *3-2-1 Goal Plan,* and your *Artist Impact List.* Do you still hold the same core values? Does your ideal community still look the same? Do the activities you're considering still make sense? Take the time to reflect on these things each year, and make sure you know what you're shooting for.

Now, let's talk about how to promote your music during creation.

12

PROMOTION DURING CREATION (PART I)

Y ou may not want to hear this, but the promotion for a release should begin during the creative process. There are three key ways this should happen.

First, promotion — community building — should actually shape what you create. I'm not saying that you should sell out and make mainstream mean-nothing pop; I'm saying the opposite. You should intentionally create music that aligns with your ideal community.

Don't balk at this. Many artists cherish the idea that they only make art for personal reasons. As I've communicated throughout this book, that's not true. Making personal art is fine — it's even necessary. But art isn't art unless it communicates something to someone else. You're reading a book about promotion, which means that, on some level, you care about other people hearing and relating to your music. So, consider what kind of music you can create that will best serve your goals in communicating your personal perspective.

This can move in many directions. Community building might shape the themes you write about. It might shape the genre you work in. It might impact the manner in which you record the songs. But it shouldn't be ignored when you create.

When Leif Vollebekk, for example, recorded "Elegy" for 2017's *Twin Solitudes*, he did so knowing the perspective he wanted to communicate: He wanted the record to be meditative. "It's funny," he told *The Village Voice*, "That was kind of the go-to word for me. The songs for this record were written in that way—in a really calm mood." He used that thematic line to guide the recording process for what would become the album's most-streamed track.

> "I tried recording it a couple of times and it was coming out like an orchestrated song. It felt really wrong, so I took a step back. The drummer was right by me, so I played the piano and sang while he played drums. We did it all live in one take."[1]

In other words, he had a vision for what he wanted to communicate, and that dictated his creative process. Listening through, it's hard to imagine the song any other way. There's an organic space to the song that'd be smothered by the sterile perfection of overproduction. Vollebekk's artistic choice was promotion in action. And it turned out beautifully.

Artists who make intentional records have an easier time building community. That might seem obvious. But it isn't; out of the 40 or so submissions I get each day to *Two Story Melody*, only about 10 are likely to have any discernible intentionality behind them. Unsurprisingly, those are often the submissions that catch my ear.

With that in mind, here are a few questions to ask as you create.

- What do I want this music to say? What are the main ideas, themes, and perspectives that it will convey?
- Who will this music speak to?
- What is the best format or medium to deliver this art?
- How should the creative process support what I want to communicate?
- If my art's potential is fully realized, what does that look like?

Personal art isn't incompatible with these questions; you should be guided in your answers by a clearly defined, personal perspective. And, as always, these considerations are simply a starting point.

The second way promotion should be incorporated into this stage is by intentionally showcasing your creative process to build artistic context.

I believe that artists are at their most interesting when they're creating. People want to see behind the scenes. Ultimately, if you can help your fans to experience your creative process, they'll have more context for your artistry and your community will be stronger.

Take, for example, Taylor Swift's promotional campaign for 2017's *Reputation*, which included a backstage look at her songwriting and production process via the AT&T-sponsored series, *The Making of a Song*. The videos in the series rely almost exclusively on footage Swift shot from her phone, often showing her working through phrasing and melodies with nonsense words or manipulating backing tracks with producers in-studio. Frankly, whether you love Taylor Swift or you can't stand her, it's fascinating.

Watching her songs develop in awkward starts and stops, you feel like you know Swift better — like her megastar facade has been dropped and she's your normal (kind of goofy) friend. That's the point, of course. Taylor Swift is a marketing genius. The album's theme was authenticity, so Swift's team intelligently showcased the ultimate authentic act: the creative process. And if the YouTube comments are any indication, her audience loved it.

"It's so cool to watch her figure this stuff out," affirms one commenter on the video for "Delicate."

"So grateful she did this series of showing us the process," gushes another. And on and on, for more than 4,000 comments and over three million views.

The creative process is its own context. Your community will be the most interested in your work when you're creating it. Capitalize on that. Don't just promote the destination; invite your fans on the journey.

Finally, the third way you should integrate promotion into your creative process is by inviting your fans into the act of creation itself.

This isn't a necessity, and I don't think you should necessarily do it for every project you produce. But, as I've noted, shared high-value actions are often the biggest factor in building community strength. Giving you fans chances to join in as you create can be hugely impactful.

The most obvious tactic toward this for indie artists is crowdfunding. I'm not going to exhaustively cover how to crowdfund here, but I'd like to provide five quick thoughts for your consideration.

First, crowdfunding is one of the most impactful ways you can invite your community to act in support of your music. That fact alone makes it valuable, even if you're blessed to be able to afford the music production process out-of-pocket.

Second, crowdfunding is difficult to sustain. You can crowdfund multiple projects, but you can't crowdfund every album. In Kickstarter's name, they drive the idea across: Crowdfunding is meant to be a kickstart — a launching point — not a sustained mechanism for income. At some point, your community will expect you to have "made it."

Third, the sweet spot for running a crowdfunding campaign is the point where you've built up a small but highly engaged audience. This means that you have fans on the basis of low-budget art and you're ready to create art at the next level. If you don't have fans, don't crowdfund. In your marketing funnel, crowdfunding is at the bottom; it's a conversion piece that drives action. You shouldn't expect to capture new fans with a crowdfunding campaign, and you shouldn't expect to turn people who've heard of you into fans. But you should expect to turn fans into die-hards; you should expect to both benefit from and increase your existing community's strength.

Fourth, if you do crowdfund, do it on Kickstarter. According to Crowdfundinsider.com, "Kickstarter success rate averages 43.4%, while Indiegogo stands at 9.8%."[2] They go on to note that the "Indiegogo success rate jumps to 17.1% for fixed funding, but 95.6% of campaigns are 'flex funding.'" The all-or-nothing nature of Kickstarter gives your fans more incentive to participate and actually makes your campaign more likely to succeed.

Fifth, the most effective crowdfunding tactic is to reach out personally to 30-50 of your biggest fans. I've mentioned the Pareto Principle before, and it comes into play here, too: 80% of crowdfunding donations come from 20% of donors. If you reach a goal of $10,000, $8,000 of that will come in big chunks from your big fans. So, work to get them involved at a personal level; use email, direct message, text, phone calls — whatever is appropriate in your personal relationship. If you're like most indie artists, you probably know most of these people as friends or even family. That's okay. Actually, it's the best place to start.

So, to recap how promotion fits into the creation of music:

Promotion should shape what you create. You should showcase your creative process as its own context. And you should look for ways to get your community involved via actions that support your creative process.

Now, let's take a look at how those guidelines can play out on your platforms.

13

PROMOTION DURING CREATION
(PART II)

I t's time to talk tactics. I'm going to go nuts-and-bolts here and lay out the platforms I recommend you use during creation and a simple approach to use on each.

Let's start with my favorite: email.

How to Use Your Email List During Creation

When we covered email as a platform, I noted that it should be the primary way you communicate to your core audience of fans and that it will be one of your biggest means of inspiring your fans to action. Accordingly, during this stage of the release process, you should use email in two ways:

First, use it to showcase what's happening "backstage." You can do this on other platforms, too (Instagram stories come to mind), but there's a level of intimacy in email that's different from other platforms. Unless you've made your profile private (and you shouldn't), anyone can see your Instagram story; only your fans get your emails. It's like a secret club. Treat it that way, and bring them into the process.

The approach I recommend is the weekly studio diary. As you're moving through the creative process, send out a weekly email that gives an update on your progress, your latest thoughts on the record or life, a random story from the week, a password-protected link to the latest demo from the project, or all of the above. Pick a date and a time to send your email each week, and stick to that schedule as much as you're able to so that it becomes something your fans look forward to.

If you're able to stick to a schedule, preface your subject line with something consistent. For example: "Studio Stories: My drummer is insane..." one week, "Studio Stories: Vocal tracking is done!" another. Consistent branding and timing will generally increase your open rates, especially if you're taking the time to actually write good stuff.

Finally, you should include one direct call-to-action in each email you send so that you always give your readers something to do. This doesn't always have to be a huge ask. You could, for example, end your email with a conversational question and ask fans to reply with their answers. At the next level up, you could encourage actions that support the creative process — maybe send out a survey on song names after sending out a link to the demo. You can always, of course, encourage merch buying. The possibilities are limitless, but make sure you're encouraging *something,* and make it something that aligns with your community.

From a metric perspective, during a campaign, you should track your open rates and click-through rates. Generally, you should expect at least 30% of your list to open your email and at least 2-5% of them to take the action you encourage — but the higher you raise those rates, the better. (You can raise them by consistently creating emails that express your perspective effectively.)

How to Use Your Website During Creation

The next platform we'll focus on is your website.

Good news here: During the creation stage, not too much is required on your site. You'll likely want to use your homepage to promote your upcoming art (although if you recently released something — say within the last three months — you may want to leave that as your featured work for now).

When you have your photoshoot (this will usually happen after you're done creating, but you never know), update your above-the-fold imagery to any project-relevant artwork that you have. You should be showcasing your newsletter signup here, too; make sure to explain that you're running a weekly email while you're in the creative process.

I also recommend including a link to a previous email near your signup form with text that says something like, "See an example of what you're missing." You can grab web links of your emails from your mail provider, and it's an effective way to incentivize signups — again, especially if you're taking the time to write good emails.

The only other tactic I recommend here is blogging. First, you should create a blog post announcing the start of your new project. If you can, pin this to your homepage or in a featured section on your blog.

From there, your blog posts can overlap with your email content, but they should be at least slightly different, because, again, an email list is private, while anyone can visit your site.

Do this a few times a month, and put your favorite updates here — the studio diary entries you're most proud of. Don't link demos and don't worry too much about incentivizing actions (other than, maybe, encouraging email signups).

The metric to track during this stage is still the number of users to your site per month.

How to Use Your Social Channels During Creation

The only other platforms I recommend using during the creation phase are your social channels.

For general posting, stick to your *Posting Playbook,* and remember that you can duplicate content from Instagram to Facebook. As you're doing so, focus the majority of your content around studio time and your creative process. The biggest key is to make sure that your audience knows that the journey toward the new project is underway — and that they're invited along for the ride.

You should also use Instagram Stories during this phase. You'll have to feel out your own approach to stay authentic to your personality and your community's vibe, but I've found that the weekly diary tactic plays well here, too. In general, take a similar approach on your Stories as you do via email and show-case "backstage" contexts.

A difference, though, is that a weekly Instagram Story is at the low end of the frequency spectrum; it's best, from an engagement perspective, to update your Story multiple times every day. (Personally, I hate the idea of being tied to my phone that much, but if you don't, then do it.)

Really, the only additional guidance I have is that you should hone your perspective and then put it on full display. The possibilities are literally endless as long as you're reflecting your views as an artist.

Know what you stand for and then be yourself.

The metrics to track on your social channels will remain the same during this period: Just keep tabs on your numbers of followers.

14

PROMOTION TO PREPARE FOR THE RELEASE (PART I)

W e've finally arrived at the phase most people think of when they think of music promotion: the preparation for a release.

This is the phase where your music exists in some form and you're starting to think about how you'll get it heard and engaged with. It doesn't necessarily have to exist as a fully mastered and mixed piece, but you'll at least need a demo version of your work to engage in any of the activities included here.

The main focus of this phase should be to build excitement within your existing community and to lay the foundation for growing your community; while you'll be doing outreach, community growth won't happen in earnest until the music is out.

One of the most common questions I get asked is, "How long should I give myself to prepare for a release?" In other words, people want to know how much lead time is needed for good promotion to happen during this phase — and, at the same time, most people just want to put their music out as quickly as they can. It makes sense. Waiting sucks, especially when you've finally finished your music after pouring so much effort into it.

Here's the answer: The best time frame for pre-release promotion is to give yourself three months before release. This is enough time for promotional work to not feel rushed; you can spend two months on prep-work to make sure everything is in order, then nail outreach in the third month.

If you want to seriously promote your music, one month is the absolute minimum amount of lead time to give before release. You'll see why as we work through these activities — there's a lot to do, and if you move any faster than that, you'll absolutely be shortchanging yourself and sabotaging your results.

So, let's get into it. Here are the activities you should do as you get ready to release your music:

1. Create an EPK
2. Run a press coverage campaign to get a premiere
3. Run a SubmitHub campaign for blog and playlist placements
4. Run a Spotify pre-save campaign
5. Prepare your song for Spotify
6. Continue backstage emails and social posts

Over the next pages, I'll cover each in more depth.

Prep Work: Create an EPK

The first thing you'll need to do is the prep work of building context for your music. It's time to build your electronic press kit — or, as it's affectionately known in acronym form, an *EPK*.

An *EPK* is a collection of materials that couch your music into your bigger context as an artist. It should tell the story of your music cohesively and quickly, emphasizing the unique elements of your artistry to generate interest. It's used to pitch your music for coverage; you'll be sending your *EPK* to press outlets you'd like to be featured in. It's also a helpful tool toward framing your own story. Taking the time to craft an *EPK* can help you to contextualize your music and artistry more effectively.

*EPK*s should include:

- The link to your song
- Your artist bio
- Your press release
- Your brief
- Artist photos
- Music artwork
- Links to relevant (standout) press coverage
- Links to your social profiles
- Your contact information

As I've mentioned before, I recommend using SoundCloud for sharing your music with industry contacts. Upload your track there, make it private, and use the private link in your *EPK*. Lead with this link, because the primary point of your *EPK* is to get people to listen to your music.

We covered photos and art in Chapter 7; now, let's get into the other aspects of the *EPK*.

How to Write Your Artist Bio

Your artist bio will be used on your website and on your music platforms (Spotify, SoundCloud, and YouTube). It should be 300-500 words, and it should describe you as an artist in a context that's broader than your latest project.

The tone of your bio should be journalistic. It should paint your artistry in a favorable light, but it should be far more objective than promotional. Because of this, it can be helpful to get someone else to write a bio. But, if you can write well (and have no problem referring to yourself or your band in the third person), there's no reason you can't be the one to write it.

Tips

- If you're a solo artist, your bio should introduce you by full name. Subsequently, it should refer to you by last name only (when not using pronouns).
- It should be written in the third person (don't use "I" or "we").
- It should provide a little bit of backstory on your artistry — how you got into music and writing, where you're from, what you're like.
- It should mention influences or similar artists.
- It should mention previous projects, coverage (if relevant), and any accomplishments that stand out.

How to Write Your Press Release

While your bio showcases your artistry at a broader scale, your press release will focus specifically on your current project. It will be used to pitch relevant publications (blogs, playlists, magazines, etc.) for coverage of the music — you will probably be using excerpts from this in your outreach emails.

Accordingly, it should present the most interesting angle or narrative available for your music. This may involve some of your artist backstory or some specific context of this project.

The press release should be 300-500 words. Its tone should be professional with a touch of storytelling. It can be lightly promotional, but it shouldn't be gushy.

Tips:

- Lead with the most compelling narrative factor of the project.
- Incorporate one artist quote (if you're doing this yourself, you can make this up).
- If you have press, incorporate a compelling quote from existing coverage.
- Ideally, relate the conclusion to the introduction in a way that brings closure to the narrative.

The press release is especially important because publications often use this content to shape their own coverage. The lazier (worse) publications will literally copy and paste your press release if they cover you. Know this going in, and be sure that your press release says what you want it to say about your music.

How to Write Your Artist Brief

Your artist brief essentially summarizes your artistry and latest project into three to five really compelling sentences. These sentences may (but don't have to) be copied or adapted from your artist bio or press release.

You'll use your artist brief to pitch publications for coverage; you might include it in the first lines of emails you send soliciting blog placements. It's meant to catch the eye of industry people and draw them in. If your *EPK* is a song, this is the hook.

Again, it should be as compelling as possible.

How to Package It All Together

Okay — you've got your content. For it to be useful in soliciting press coverage, you'll need to package it all together for journalists to easily review.

There are two ways that are acceptable for this. The first (and easiest) is to just put everything together into a Google doc and make it public for anyone who has the link. When you pitch publications, you'll send them that. This is increasingly popular — at *Two Story Melody*, about half of the submissions we receive are packaged in this way.

The second (and slightly more professional) way is to create an *EPK* page on your website. Essentially, you'll do the same thing — gather all of the materials and make them available via a link to your website. You can make this page password-protected; in my view, it's not necessary, and it adds an extra hoop for journalists to jump through before they stream your music.

If you're working with a promo company, they'll take care of this process for you. Many agencies will upload your EPK to their site and link journalists there.

Speaking of which, this is a book about how to promote indie music, and it's clearly directed toward artists who take a DIY approach. That said, as we get into press outlets and playlist promotion, I feel I owe it to you to briefly lay out what it's like to work with a promo company.

Don't worry. I promise this won't be a sales pitch.

15

PROMOTION TO PREPARE FOR THE RELEASE (PART II)

S hould you work with a promo company?

As I hope I've made clear, this depends on what your goals are. Promo companies have three main functions: to get your music covered (in blogs, magazines, and other publications), to get your music played (on the radio or online), and to grow your audience (usually on social platforms).

You can, of course, achieve all of these things yourself. But you may choose to work with a promo company based on one of three value propositions:

First, they have time. This is a commodity, but there is value in it all the same. If you work with an agency, they will dedicate time to promotion — and promotion does take time. To do this stage of promotion well typically takes *a lot* of time. If you'd prefer not to spend time on this yourself, you may choose to hire someone.

Second, they have broader experience. Artists who do promotion themselves are left to work through the trial and error of tactics based on their own small sample size; it's as if they're studying probability by flipping one coin ten times while an agency has the ability to flip ten coins at once.

Agencies work with more artists, and so they can get a better feel for the tactics that work consistently: how to structure EPKs, how to set up press campaigns, how to manage playlist promotion, and social ads, and so on. This experience can (but doesn't always) lead to increased effectiveness. A good question to ask a potential agency is: How will you do this service better than I could do it myself?

Third, and most importantly, agencies have connections. In my opinion, this is the main value you get in working with an agency: You pay for a boost in your artist foundation of connection by capitalizing on theirs. You may not know the editor at *Consequence of Sound* or *Rolling Stone* or *Billboard* or whatever. The best agencies do. This doesn't guarantee that they'll get you coverage in those places (anybody who guarantees coverage at a specific place is scamming you), but it vastly improves your chances of those places actually hearing your music.

With all of that said, let's return to the question: Should you work with an agency?

For the likely majority of artists reading this book, the answer is probably: not yet.

My advice is to work with an agency *after* doing promotional work yourself. This is especially true with any type of work that doesn't require you to spend much of your own money — things like press or playlist outreach. Again, social ads are a bit more of a risk, because doing them without experience is a bit like gambling, but I still think you should start small and try things yourself.

This way, you'll give a future agency something to build from; it's easier to get a placement with *Consequence of Sound* when you've been covered by mid-tier publications before. And, more importantly, if you do promo work yourself, you'll have a better idea of what you're looking for help with, instead of approaching promotion as some kind of magic that happens behind a curtain — a view that's all-too-common and often leads to artists getting ripped off.

With that clarified, it's time to walk through one of the promo activities agencies are often enlisted for help with: the accumulation of press coverage.

How to Think About Press Coverage

One of my primary functions at Two Story Media is to help artists get press coverage for new music. Most artists come to me with some idea that press is a good thing, but not many come with an understanding of why. In other words, they don't have clear goals. That's a problem, but it's easily solved: You can create clear goals if you consider how press coverage should support your community.

There are a few ways that should happen — but the main purpose in pursuing press coverage may not be what you think it is.

Artists often view press coverage primarily as a means of expanding their audience. The idea is that, if you're covered somewhere, you'll reach that publication's audience, and some of those people will become your fans. Get covered in *Atwood*

Magazine, for example, and some of the magazine's regular readers will probably start following you.

There's a problem with that premise, though. These days, very few music publications have a significant audience of regular readers.

Most music press outlets work the other way. They use artists' audiences to create the facade of their own. At *Two Story Melody,* for example, only 14% of our website visitors are returning viewers. The vast majority of the traffic we get is correlated to the artists we write about. In other words: We cover an artist. The artist is pumped about the coverage and promotes it on their platforms. Their audience heads to our site to read the piece. Then everyone goes their separate ways; we write about other music, and most of the artist's fans never return to *Two Story Melody.*

True, we do have our own community. We have an email list of several thousand people who get our coverage each month. There are music industry people who keep tabs on our site. But, in general, coverage with us — and with most music publications — is not a way to *significantly* grow your audience. The only outlets where this is an exception are the very top-tier places: *Rolling Stone* or *Pitchfork* or *The New York Times.* Even these outlets, though, are primarily read by people interested in the artists they cover — not by people primarily interested in the outlets themselves.

You will reach more people if you're covered in a lot of places, but press coverage is a fairly ineffective way to reach new fans.

So, instead of building audience size, press coverage serves the primary purpose of building your artist context (which, as you'll remember from Chapter 7, is correlated to the marketing funnel stage of interest). Press coverage makes you more interesting to your fans; it gives them something to read about you and another way to consume your art.

I liken it to sports fanship. I'm a Steelers fan. I'm only a little sorry. One of the rituals I perform as a Steelers fan is to read news about the team, and reading that news actually makes me more engaged in my fanship. When I read coverage, I think about the team more. I talk about them more. Coverage makes me a bigger fan (and probably a more annoying one). In the same way, music press coverage gives your fans a place and a practice to become bigger fans. It strengthens your community around your artist context.

Second, press coverage builds your credibility. It can help you to get opportunities down the line. When you submit your music to other publications, you can quote excerpts from existing coverage as proof that your music is good. When you reach out to venues, you can do this, too. It's social proof, and, as we've seen in thinking about contagion theory, social proof helps to open doors.

Third, press coverage does help to position your music on listening platforms. Spotify, for example, uses natural language processing to scan the web for mentions of songs and artists, then filters coverage through an algorithm to identify descriptive words or related artists. This information is one factor they use to place your music. It impacts their decision to place you in Release Radar or Discover Weekly playlists, for example, and influences which Related Artists show on your profile. (While this can certainly lead to new fans, it's just one factor out of many that Spotify uses to sort your music and shouldn't be used as a primary growth tool.)

The bottom line here is that press coverage is valuable, but it will not help you to get more fans right now — at least in a very significant way. Use it to build your community pillar of context and pursue it accordingly.

How to Run a Press Coverage Campaign for a Premiere

It's time to get tactical again. With an understanding of what press coverage is for, here's how you should run a campaign to start getting covered.

First, review and refine your list of comparable artists.

This list will serve as a centering point for many of your promotional activities. In press coverage, it will help you to identify outlets to submit to. First, though, make sure that it's up-to-date. In Chapter 6, we discussed how to get feedback. You should repeat this process for any new music that you're considering promoting. What artists do people liken you to? Are the artists on your list still representative of the music you're making? Remove any artists that are no longer relevant, and add any that are.

Second, create a *Press Tracking Sheet* to track the publications you'll pitch.

The spreadsheet should include the following columns: Publication, Coverage Type, Date Submitted, Date of Follow-Up, Coverage Status, and Notes.

Publication	Type	Submission	Follow-Up	Status	Notes
Pitchfork	Premiere	7/10/20	7/17/20	Rejected	Harsh feedback

Create a spreadsheet like this. Maybe pass on submitting to Pitchfork.

You can add columns if you'd like to track more (like, say, the emails of individual contacts at each publication), but this is a good template to start with. Note that it's worth it to link each publication to its website.

Third, use this spreadsheet to create a list of 20 to 30 publications to target for a premiere of your music.

The strategy is this: Pitching a publication with a premiere opportunity adds a slight bit of incentive for that publication to cover you. A premiere is the exclusive right to introduce a song. As an artist, you agree not to seek coverage elsewhere for a period of time (usually the weekend after the release), and you typically provide some kind of exclusive content (like an interview or a quote) that makes the coverage unique.

Publications — especially music blogs — want to be on the cutting edge of music discovery, so, assuming your music is good, offering outlets the chance at a premiere gives them an opportunity to make a bit of a name for themselves by breaking new music. For you, it's a way to increase your odds of getting covered.

It's okay to offer multiple outlets a premiere opportunity simultaneously — but, as soon as someone responds, you'll need to make a decision whether or not to premiere with them.

Now, how should you build your list of publications to submit to — and how can you find contact information (email addresses) so that you can reach out?

Here's what I recommend: Consult your list of comparable artists. For each artist on the list, google their name and their latest release to find where they've recently been covered. If you find three publications for every artist on the list, you'll have 30 publications to submit to. When you're seeking a premiere, set your sights high. Don't list publications if you'd be dissatisfied with their premiere coverage. Opt for the higher-level outlets you'd be proud to get covered in. I'll discuss how to submit to mid-level blogs later.

You may be able to find contact information for these top-level outlets listed on their websites. If you can't — or if you simply want to save yourself a lot of time — I recommend using The Music Industry Connection. This is basically a database of music industry contact information, and it costs 9.99 a month to subscribe to. They have the email address for almost any editor at any publication you can think of. (The Indie Bible is another compilation of contact info, but their model includes a one-time fee that's more expensive and their search engine is a little harder to use.)

You can search your database by publication name to find contacts. Yes, that means you can find the emails of editors at *Rolling Stone* and *Billboard* and *Huffington Post* and whatever else. The bigger outlets, of course, have multiple editors and writers, so instead of submitting to whoever you find first, do a bit of follow-up research and make sure you're submitting to the person(s) who will be most likely to respond to your music.

Fourth, send each contact an email. Ideally, you should make first contact a month before your release date.

If you worked through email setup in Chapter 7, you should have an email address set up from your artist domain (name@your-website.com); this looks a lot more professional than name@gmail.com. During a coverage campaign, I recommend going one step further: Create an email account specifically for press coverage (i.e. "press@your-website.com") and use it for outreach. This will cost $5 per month for as long as you use it, and it adds an additional layer of credibility to your campaign.

In each email, you should communicate that you've done your research and know what the outlet is about.

You'd be surprised how few artists do this. At *Two Story Melody*, we get a lot of mass-targeted, copy-and-paste submissions that are sent with no regard for the platform we've built: "Please consider this song for review," with no other context. That's fine, but it also doesn't give much of a reason to actually consider the song. Or, worse but funnier, "Hey, I love the heavy metal work you guys feature. Please consider covering..." (We don't tend to feature heavy metal. I mean, we might, but it's definitely not a staple).

To get things right:

- Read each outlet's About page and Submission guidelines before you submit to them.
- Refer to the outlet's coverage of your comparable artist. If you're emailing an individual writer, reference examples of their work, specifically.
- Provide the most compelling narrative angle for coverage of your music. This is usually your Artist Brief.
- Offer the outlet a premiere opportunity for the music you're pitching.
- Make sure that you mention the date of release (which is when you'd like premiere coverage to run).
- Send the full URL to your track on SoundCloud.
- Send the full URL to your EPK.

Your entire email shouldn't include more than four or five paragraphs. Here's an example:

> Hey [*Editor's Real Name*],
>
> Really appreciate your coverage at [*Outlet Name*]. I loved the write-up on [*Comparable Artist*], and I think my music is similar because [*A Good Reason*]. I'd like to offer you the opportunity to premiere my new song, [*Song Name*]. It's out next month on [*Release Date*].
>
> Here's a link to the pre-released track on SoundCloud: SoundCloud.com/private-link-to-your-track
>
> Here's a little more info about [*Artist Name*]: [*Artist Brief*].
>
> And here's a link to the full EPK: drive.google.com/your-epk
>
> Would you be interested in premiering this?
>
> Thanks again for the great work you do! Hope to hear from you soon.
>
> -Future You

Track each submission in your pitching spreadsheet. When someone responds, record their response. If you're in this for the long haul (and you are), you'll start to develop relationships with these people, and it will make securing future coverage easier.

If you get rejections, don't worry. The sad truth of this industry is that a normal success rate is 3-5%. That means that, for every 100 blogs you submit to, you can expect to get placed in three to five. The response rate for premieres is slightly higher, but in most cases, you'll only get a few positive responses out of your 20 or 30 submissions. That's true even if you're submitting the modern day equivalent of "Hey Jude" (which you are, of course).

When you get a positive response, you'll need to make a decision: Will you accept it? The vast majority of the time, you should, even if you're holding out hope for coverage with another publication you like more. A premiere is only one instance of coverage; it doesn't preclude you from being covered elsewhere after the period of exclusivity is over. Actually, it makes you more likely to be covered elsewhere.

Here's how to make that happen: When you do accept a premiere opportunity, you should immediately reach back out to every outlet you've already emailed to let them know where you're being covered. Use this as an opportunity to reframe your coverage request.

> Hey [*Editor Name*], just following up here to let you know that [*Premiere Outlet Name*] has chosen to premiere [*Song Name*]. The track will be exclusive to them for the weekend of [*Release Date*].
>
> If you'd be interested in covering it after that, let me know. We could definitely set up an interview or provide exclusive content.
>
> Thanks!
>
> -Further in the Future You

Essentially, this is a chance to add social proof to your pitch; often, the outlets that ignored your first outreach will respond when they find out someone else is covering your music.

Fifth, if you don't get any responses, follow up. Over 50% of coverage comes after the first contact.

You should check in three times before your release, once on the day-of, and one time after. That's five touch points total. You can do more follow-ups, but past those touch points, it gets tough to balance results against the fact that you're being pretty annoying. Check back in when you have new music, but let things be for now.

And get ready to move on to another method of getting coverage: SubmitHub.

How to Run a SubmitHub Campaign

If you aren't familiar with SubmitHub, you should be.

Founded by Jason Grishkoff in 2015, the platform solves two of the indie music industry's major problems. For platforms (bloggers, labels, playlisters, and influencers), it streamlines the music submission process and keeps email inboxes from becoming overwhelming. At Two Story Melody, for example, we get about 20 to 50 artist submissions each day. If these were all emails — and they used to be — sorting through them would be a nightmare. SubmitHub makes the process of curating music much more manageable.

For artists, SubmitHub provides guaranteed access to industry folks. In other words, you can ensure that your song actually gets heard instead of sending it into the black hole of some editor's inbox. (Editors' inboxes are, in fact, black holes.)

What's the catch? Well, you've basically got to pay to play. While you can submit to platforms for free, free submissions have a significantly lower approval rate (about 5% compared to 14% for premium submissions). You'll want to buy credits, because they incentivize platforms to respond.

Here's how it works: Artists purchase premium credits for roughly $1 each (although there are bulk discounts which you should take advantage of). Platforms set their own submission price at one, two, or three credits per song. Artists use their credits to submit. When the platform reviews a track, they get to keep at least half of the submission price (so, if they've set submissions at two credits, for example, they'd make $1 for every song they listen to).

As an artist, you can choose two modes of review. Either the curator has to listen to at least 20 seconds of your song and provide at least 10 words of feedback, or they can listen to 90 seconds of your song without providing feedback. Again, the big win from the artist side is that you're guaranteed to get someone engaging with your music.

You are *not* guaranteed to get coverage, though, which is what distinguishes SubmitHub from payola schemes. There are scams out there that promise coverage in exchange for payment. SubmitHub is not one of them. It's fair, transparent, and a great idea that I wish I'd thought of before Jason.

So, how should you use SubmitHub in the lead-up to your release?

I recommend using it primarily as a place to seek mid-level blog coverage and playlist placements. Here's why: While top-tier publications (i.e. *Rolling Stone, Billboard, Pitchfork*) work almost exclusively on a more relational basis, smaller outlet outreach is incredibly efficient on SubmitHub.

Other options for getting playlist placements are either more expensive or straight-up scammy. Other options for targeting small blogs are either more expensive or far more time-consuming. SubmitHub works for both of these things, and you can do it yourself at a really affordable cost without spending copious amounts of time.

Here's how I recommend running your pre-release campaign.

You'll obviously need to create a SubmitHub profile and upload the song you'll be promoting. (SubmitHub can pull from SoundCloud, so all you'll need to do is add that link.) Follow the guidelines — you'll add your artwork, similar artists, and a brief description of the track. All of this is straightforward, and, honestly, what matters more than any of the meta info you add is your song itself. Unlike traditional email promotion — where your pitch is the gateway to getting someone to listen — SubmitHub ensures your song will get played. For the most part, if it's good, curators will engage with it, and if it's not, it won't matter what you say about it.

My one caveat to this is that, if your song starts slowly, you should say so, and you should specifically mention where it picks up. Curators can decline your song after 20 seconds, but if you say something like, "The first chorus at 0:45 will hit you hard," they're more likely to listen till that point.

Once you've gotten your song set up, it's time to purchase credits. If you have the budget, you should opt for the bulk-purchase of 100 credits for $80. This is the best bargain on the site, and if you get a platform-standard placement rate, it'll translate to about 10 or 12 placements.

When you're ready to submit your song, SubmitHub will walk you through a few screens to help you select the right settings for your campaign. You should choose these options:

- You'll be asked whether you want to submit via

standard or premium credits. Choose the premium credit option.

- You'll be asked how much you care about getting feedback on your song. Choose "Feedback is very important to me." Curators are more likely to engage with your song — and to listen to more of it — if you select this option.
- You'll be asked about the copyright on your song. Keep the copyright to yourself. You'll be looking for blog coverage and Spotify placements, and, for the most part, copyright shouldn't affect those.
- You'll be asked to pick genres that your song fits into. Choose the three genres that you feel are most applicable to the specific track you're promoting.

Those settings should complete the wizard. From there, you'll be brought to a screen where you can filter through different blogs and curators.

First, you should focus on submitting to blogs in your genre that also curate Spotify playlists. Many of these outlets, if they write about you, will also include you in their playlist, so getting their approval means two placements for the effort of one.

If you've used SubmitHub for previous campaigns, you should also resend to any outlets that have covered you before. (On this note: You should "Favorite" anyone that covers you. This will make repeat submissions easy, because there's an option to filter for your "Favorites".

Once you've cleared those contacts out, filter for what SubmitHub calls "Really Good Bloggers." These are blogs that will write about your music, as opposed to just copying and pasting your press release.

Finally, just work your way through your screen of genre-relevant curators. I recommend paying special attention to Approval Rate, and submitting to outlets that fall between 5% and 30%. Why? Well, if you submit to outlets that approve less than 5% of submissions, you're masochistic and are obviously setting yourself up for disappointment. On the other side, though, if you submit to the outlets that approve more than 30% of submissions, your placements won't mean much. SubmitHub has what's essentially a chart of popular music on the platform, and approvals at outlets with over a 30% approval rate don't count toward getting your music on it.

Additionally, if you submit to outlets that take virtually anything, you might get lumped in with artists that don't match your vibe or that just make bad music. This can jack up algorithmic perceptions of your songs.

An approval rate of between 5% and 30% is the sweet spot for getting a decent number of placements at respectable outlets.

After you submit, you wait. You deal with a lot of poorly-thought-out rejections from people who would probably call "Bohemian Rhapsody" "kind of cool but a little too experimental for my taste." And, ultimately, you get to celebrate a hopefully encouraging number of meaningful placements.

It's a lot to go through, but it's worth it.

How to Prepare Your Song for Spotify

It's time to talk about Spotify again.

We both know that you want streams. I've made the case that streams aren't everything — and it's true — but, still, you want them. They're validation that people are listening to your music, they're a (sadly inefficient) means of generating income from your art, and, most importantly, they're a means of building your community. So, let's get streams.

Despite what you might have heard, the path toward streams isn't overly complex. There are four basic means of generating them: through your own existing fans and Spotify followers, through placements on user-created playlists, through placements on Spotify-generated playlists, and through ad campaigns (which aren't relevant until after your music is released).

You have the least control over landing on Spotify-generated playlists, but I'd like to start there, because it requires little of you and because understanding how Spotify-generated playlists work is a good introduction into the platform's functionality.

So, how do Spotify-generated playlists work?

The answer depends on the playlist. Spotify runs two kinds of playlists: personal and editorial. The personal playlists are algorithmically generated for individual Spotify listeners. By and large, the editorial playlists are curated by real human beings who work for Spotify. Let's tackle personal playlists first.

How the Spotify Algorithm Works

The entire point of the Spotify algorithm is to serve listeners music they'll like. Doing this effectively is what keeps people listening to Spotify. To do this, the Spotify algorithm relies on two main types of data points: music data and user data. There are several key ways that these data points are plotted out.

Music is contextualized against other music. In other words, Spotify is able to determine that Kendrick Lamar sounds (at least a little bit) similar to J. Cole, which is why you'll see each artist appear under the other's "Fans Also Like" tab. More importantly for our purposes here, Spotify also does this on a song-by-song basis. They can plot out that "Watermelon Sugar" and "Sunday Best" are similar enough to be included on a Summer Hits playlist, for example, while excluding Harry Styles' "Falling".

Users are also contextualized against each other. Spotify is able to take all user listening data and plot out individual's tastes and habits based on comparisons against other users. Let's say, for example, you listen to J. Cole and Kendrick Lamar and also frequently stream the playlist Jazz Vibes. Based on that information, Spotify knows that your profile is similar to Frank's (who, like you, likes mainstream rap and has poor taste in jazz). Because your profiles are similar, when Frank starts listening to new artist DJ Piper, Spotify assumes that there's a good chance you'll like DJ Piper, too. So, the platform places a DJ Piper track in a personalized playlist for you to discover.

And that's where the rubber meets the road – in the pairing of music with users based on all of that data.

What does this mean for you? Really, it only means one thing: If you want your song to be placed in Spotify's algorithmic (personalized) playlists, you need your song to accumulate as much data as possible so that Spotify can determine where to place it in all of this. The more data your music has, the more likely it is to show up in the places people listen, because Spotify will know where to put it.

There are three ways for your song to accumulate data. The first is the most obvious: Spotify activity, meaning streams, song saves, and playlist placements. The more users stream your track, the better Spotify will determine what kind of users like it, and the better they'll be able to recommend it to similarly profiled users. The more users favorite, save, and playlist your music, the more Spotify can determine how it's grouped; if your mom puts it on her "My Favorite Summer Jams EVER!" playlist, Spotify will assume that you're somehow summer-y and similar to the other music included there (so let's hope your mom has good taste and understands what summer sounds like). This is also why you should avoid playlisting scams and bot streams; they'll ruin your data profile and keep you from showing up in the right places.

We've mentioned the second way for your song to accumulate data before: natural language processing. Spotify, like Google, constantly crawls the web for mentions of music and artists. When your song gets covered in blogs, Spotify analyzes the language of the coverage to contextualize your song. If the writer called it "80s-inspired, bright, and chippy," maybe you'll end up next to Wham!. If they called it "somber and heavy," maybe you'll end up next to Hozier. The more coverage you get, the more Spotify can contextualize your music, and the more likely you'll be to get placed in algorithmic playlists.

The third way Spotify gets data on your song is, literally, through the song's data. Some of this you input manually. On Spotify for Artists, you can specify your music's genre and some additional metadata like descriptions and credit info. Spotify also looks at the actual sound profile of your song; they can automatically determine things like what key it's in, its BPM, and how compressed it is. They'll factor in all of this information when deciding if and where to place your song.

How Spotify Editorial Playlists Work

Algorithmic playlists are auto-generated; editorial playlists are (for the most part) made by real humans who work at Spotify.

These people filter through songs and put them together into thousands of regularly updated playlists. Often, editorial playlists have a huge audience. Fresh Finds, which tends to feature new music from up-and-coming artists, has over 700,000 followers. Rap Caviar has over 13 million. Hot Country has nearly 6 million. Indie Pop has about 1 million. You get the idea. These are the kinds of placements that can skyrocket your streams. That doesn't *necessarily* translate toward you building a sustainable community, but it can help.

So, how do you get on Spotify editorial playlists? You prepare your music for Spotify and hope you get picked.

At the most basic level, that means that you use your Spotify for Artists account to submit your new music for playlist consideration. This is incredibly easy to do. First, when you upload your new music to your distributor, you need to set a release date that's in the future. Do not choose immediate release. This is very important. I recommend scheduling out your release at least a month into the future; ideally, you should opt to release your song five or six weeks out. That timeframe will give your distributor and Spotify enough time to process your music.

When your distributor has successfully submitted your music to Spotify, you'll see it appear in your Spotify for Artists profile under the tab "Upcoming." This is where you'll be able to submit it for editorial playlist consideration.

The submission process is pretty straightforward. From that tab, just follow Spotify's wizard, and be as detailed and accurate as possible about your song information when you submit it.

And that's it.

Now, there's nothing you can do to guarantee official Spotify playlist placements. But the more data you can generate for your song, the more likely it'll be that Spotify places you somewhere. That's true for both algorithmically and editorially created playlists; editors consider your song's data, too. So, once you've submitted your music, you should focus on generating data.

One way to do that is through blog coverage and user playlist placement, which we've just discussed.

The other way to do that is through getting pre-saves of your song before its release.

Let's talk through how to do that next.

How to Run a Spotify Pre-Save Campaign

The purpose of a pre-save campaign is, as its name suggests, to get people to save your track on Spotify before it's released. The people who pre-save your music should have it appear in their personalized Release Radar or Discover Weekly playlists when it's out. And, importantly, when users pre-save your music, your music accumulates data, and Spotify can start to figure out who else they should show it to. All of this makes you more likely to land on Spotify playlists.

At a basic level, running a Spotify pre-save campaign is pretty simple: You get a link that, when clicked, will let users pre-save your music. You send this link to your community. They click it. And that's that. I'll break all of this down into more detail, but those are the general steps.

The foundational step, of course, is to get your pre-save link. This can actually be a bit complicated, and here's why: "Pre-save" is not an official Spotify functionality. When you run a pre-save campaign, what happens on a technical level is that the platform you choose actually acts on the behalf of Spotify users to automatically favorite the song immediately after it's released. This involves some developer-heavy stuff, like integrating with Spotify's API. It's not just copy-pasting a link.

This is a little bit convoluted, but it's still worth it.

The exact process will vary a bit depending on what platform you use for it. If you've distributed via DistroKid, you'll want to use HyperFollow to create this (it's free and built into Distro-Kid). On CDBaby, you'll probably want to use Show.co (which is free if you're a CDBaby member). If you aren't on either of those distributors, you can try SmartURL, which is free for anyone but a little bit clunky aesthetically.

On several of these marketing platforms, the key to generating the right link is to get a number for your song called a URI. This is where things get a little complicated. Currently, you can find this through a hack: Under your Upcoming tab, if you click the three dots next to your music and click "View Playlist Pitch," you'll be taken to a screen where your Spotify URI is in your URL. Go up to your browser window and grab the code immediately following /submission/. That's your URI.

Yes, this is an obnoxious process. My bet is that this gets updated so that it's built directly into Spotify soon.

Most of the marketing platforms don't give you a ton of leeway in designing your landing page; they'll simply generate one for you using the assets you provide. Use the best narrative angle for your song that you can (probably your artist brief) and upload your song artwork, and that's pretty much it. Now, you've got a page to send people to where they can hit the pre-save button.

It's time to send it to your community. And that brings us to our final pre-release tactic.

How to Use Your Platforms During Pre-Release

Hopefully, you've begun to build the foundation for your community at this point. Now, it's time to tap into it. While many artists are concerned with audience growth during the pre-release stage, you should focus most heavily on reaching your existing community during this period.

Relatedly, I don't recommend doing paid advertising during pre-release. Some artists run paid campaigns for Spotify pre-saves. I've found that, generally, the costs-per-click for this tactic are too high to make it appealing. When the song is out, you can use it to grow your community. For now, focus on the platforms you've built.

The possibilities on your platforms are always limitless — really, as I've said too many times at this point, as long as you're representing your well-defined perspective to your audience and consistently communicating about your project, you'll do okay. I do recommend two things, though.

First of all, update all of your platforms to clearly communicate your upcoming release date and display your Spotify pre-save link. These two things should become the most prominent pieces of info on your website; they should be in your Instagram bio; you should get them tattooed somewhere near your eyebrows.

When your fans engage with your artistry on any of your platforms, they should immediately realize you have new music coming out.

Second, on both email and social, put together a branded campaign in the month leading up to your release date that's focused on building awareness for the project. Again, the point is to make sure that everyone in your community knows when your song is coming out.

On social, this might look like themed bi-weekly posts sharing interesting anecdotes about the project. Make the theme fairly obvious. I love when artists use the same background on Insta posts, for example, or when they have a common color palette for every post about an album.

Via email, a branded campaign should include at least a weekly send each of the four weeks prior to release. The emails should have similarly-titled subject lines, should be authentic to your perspective, and should include the release data and pre-save link. The content angles are limitless, but keep a consistent message and aesthetic and incorporate the pillars of community.

In general, you should focus on encouraging action; whether it's attending the release show or simply hitting the pre-save link, the more your community acts in support of your artistry, the more committed your community will be. Give your fans opportunities to act as release day approaches.

And get ready. When your song is out, the party really starts.

16

PROMOTION FOR THE RELEASE

I t's release day! The party's really starting.

Congratulations. If you've made it this far, you've arrived at the moment you've been waiting and working for: You've got new music going live. Now, it's time to get it heard by people who will care about it.

I'm going to break this phase up into two sub-phases: the promotion you should do immediately on the day of release, and the promotion you should do for the month after the song is out.

Let's start with the promotion on the day of release.

Release Day Checklist

First, you should immediately update all of your platforms to reflect the fact that your music has reached the world.

That will mean creating a link for easy listening. Believe it or not, some people listen to music on platforms other than Spotify. It'd be a shame for your audience to hit your link only to end up at a platform they don't use. So, as discussed in Chapter 7, you should create a landing page with links to every platform the music can be streamed from. Again, you can do this via a service like linktree, but my preferred approach is to create this on your website. Link to Spotify, Apple Music, Amazon Music, YouTube, SoundCloud — basically, everywhere that your stuff is out.

As I mentioned before, I also recommend including an opt-in for your email.

Finally, make sure that your cover art is on the page so that, when the link gets shared to Facebook, the art will get pulled in and your post will look good.

With that link copied to your clipboard, it's time to update your platforms. That means that you should:

- Send an email to your list. (Include the link.)
- Create social posts for Instagram and Facebook. (Include the link.)
- Post an Instagram story. (If you're able to include the link, do it.)
- Update your website. (Put the news above the fold on your homepage.)
- Update Spotify. (Make it your artist's choice. If you built a genre-relevant playlist, add your song to the top of it. You might also consider creating an "Artist Catalogue" type of playlist — basically, just put the song at the top of a playlist of your existing music)
- Update YouTube. (Many distributors will automatically send music to YouTube. If yours doesn't, make a YouTube video by putting your music over a still of your cover art, and then upload it to your

channel. You can do lyric or music videos later.
Finally, go into your existing videos and update their descriptions to include the link to your new music on YouTube.)

Next, you should follow up with every publication you've reached out to and let them know it's live (especially if you haven't secured a premiere.)

Then you should pour a tall glass of champagne (or whiskey), kick your feet up, and toast to your hard work. Stay engaged on your platforms by responding to comments and replies, but don't wear yourself out.

You've done it.

There's more to do, but it can wait till tomorrow.

Promotion After the Release

Shake off that champagne (whiskey) and let's get back to work on building your community. Now that your song is out, the context of your artistry has grown. It's the perfect time to bring new people into the fold.

That said, you should still focus on your existing fans. The most basic thing that you should do in the month after your music is out is to engage with people as they interact with your art. Share all blog and playlist placements to your social channels (and to your email list if you think it's appropriate). Respond to people who comment on your songs. Be an active part of your artist community; your engagement will strengthen it.

That's the baseline.

The next level is where things get interesting, because it's the level where you can work to legitimately grow the size of your community. It's critical to have the right mindset here. Many artists view a release as an end goal and measure success by how well the release does. Instead, you should treat community as your end goal and use your music as an asset to build your fanbase. You've created more artist context; post-release is the time when you should focus on using that context to reach new people.

Put simply, this is the best time to consider paid ads.

Should you use paid ads? Almost definitely. In terms of promotion, paid ads are the best way to grow your audience. They allow you to show a slice of your new artist context to people who will identify with your perspective. Done right, this can quickly build your community.

So, how can you do it right? As I mentioned in Chapter 8 when discussing Facebook ads, here's what I recommend: Instead of obsessing over ad strategies, use ToneDen. No, I'm not affiliated with ToneDen. It's just a great product.

(This comes with one big caveat — if you need geographically centered fans, do the advertising yourself. ToneDen doesn't currently offer geographic targeting.)

Again, there are an endless variety of approaches in the paid ad space and a plethora of great teachers. My favorite, so far, is Indepreneur's Fan Finder method; you basically run a Video Views campaign on Facebook to mutually exclusive audiences to optimize targeting, then create a lookalike audience that's based on people who watched a percentage of your video.

This is a great approach that can get you really cost-efficient clicks. If you're interested in trying it, I'd highly recommend investing in Indepreneur; it's only $39 per month for membership to their platform where you get access to all of their courses and support from their community, all of which is really helpful.

The problem is that running a Fan Finder campaign takes a lot of work — and, even if you study the material carefully, you'll probably make some rookie mistakes (and you'll spend a lot of time making them), because Facebook's ad platform (which, remember, also powers Instagram) is complicated.

ToneDen, on the other hand, is ridiculously straightforward and comparably effective. It costs $50 per month to use the service (not including ad costs), but that's less than most courses charge, anyway, and going this route will save you a ton of time.

The platform is basically automated social ad management. In the same way that agencies are able to test and validate promo strategies with many artists at once, ToneDen is able to validate ad strategies and incorporate them into its algorithms. The result: plug-and-play ad tactics that have been really well optimized with a lot more data than you'd be able to gather yourself.

ToneDen uses what it calls "playbooks" to give you preset tracks for your campaigns. I recommend using their "Spotify Growth for Artists" playbook. It'll help you create a campaign to drive Spotify followers at very reasonable costs — likely at below $0.50 per follower, depending on your niche — using Instagram stories.

While setup is easy, there are a few things that are worth noting.

First, as discussed in Chapter 8, the three components of an ad campaign are the goal, the target, and the content. ToneDen will make setting your goal easy. But, while they'll give you a lot of direction, you'll need to help them out on the target and the content.

Target-wise, ToneDen will pull related artists from Spotify and use them for interest-based targeting. That's a good start, but it may not always be the best configuration, especially if you don't have a ton of data associated with your Spotify profile yet. So, at the very least, use the list of comparable artists that you've created to augment or adjust ToneDen's targeting. Even better: If you've run a like-generating ad campaign already (as discussed in Chapter 8), you should have a headstart on good audience data. Use it.

Content-wise, you should absolutely use a video for your ad. Video is, by far, the highest-performing content format. You don't need to do anything crazy here. You can film something yourself. You can throw your best song over free stock video from a site like Unsplash. You can use your cover art (although I'd throw a motion effect over it.) Just have something with a bit of movement, get it to look good in the vertical Instagram story format, and add clear text and direction asking users to swipe up to listen on Spotify.

ToneDen uses your ad account, so you'll be able to monitor the results yourself by logging in there. I'd recommend spending at least $50 on ads for the month after your release (although if you have the budget and the ads are working, nothing says you can't spend a lot more). If you're at $0.50 per follower, that'll net you 100 new followers — and the chances are good that you'll end up doing far better.

I'd recommend paying for growth on Instagram as a second priority during this phase. ToneDen also offers an "Instagram Growth Playbook" that's structured nearly identically to the

Spotify campaign, with the main difference being that the call-to-action leads to an Instagram follow rather than a Spotify follow. Barring something pretty weird, you can probably use the same content and targeting you applied to Spotify; just set up a campaign, put your new music to work, and start generating Instagram followers.

When (and How) to Move On

And that brings us to the final part of the promotional cycle — the end. Actually, the definition of the end is one of the most common questions I get from artists: When should I stop trying to promote my release and move onto making new music?

The answer, unfortunately, is a little demoralizing.

In the blogging and playlisting world, most releases lose their luster after the first month. One month after release, you'll find it difficult to get new placements, and the level of difficulty only increases from there. The longest you should focus on promoting one piece of art is only about three months.

Now, you can elongate this if you build more context around your work. And you should. For example, if you release a music video or a remix, you can buy yourself another month to work with. If you win a songwriting award or get some kind of accolade, you can take a second shot at promoting that achievement.

A release itself, though, is only worth actively promoting for one to three months. After that, for blogs especially, it's old news. I hate that reality, but in the world of constant tweeting and 24/7 news cycles, it's what we're stuck with.

That doesn't mean that you can't use the release in paid ads, though. In fact, if you're able to, you might consider running paid ads on a pretty consistent basis to build your followers on social platforms and Spotify. New music is slightly more exciting, but as long as you're hitting the right audience, your art will have a longer useful life in paid campaigns. And if you're consistently building your audience, you'll see a larger splash the next time you release music.

So, that's the timeline. When you do reach the end of the road, it's time to evaluate your results.

You can do a deep dive into every aspect of your promotion if you'd like to. Often, that's helpful. You should start with this, though: re-evaluating your *3-2-1 Goal Plan* and updating your *Platform Scorecard*.

Note how the numbers have changed since your last measurement and ask three questions:

- Why did the number change?
- What promotion worked?
- What promotion didn't work?

The answers to those questions should shape your strategy for the next release. If the why isn't obvious, dig into the numbers. If something worked, do more of it. If something didn't work, don't do it again.

With each cycle, you'll get better — and your community will get stronger.

NEXT STEPS

If you've made it this far: Great work, but what the heck are you still doing here? It's time to get out there.

You've read through the path toward successful promotion. Hopefully, you've considered your own path along the way, too. Now, go build your community.

It won't happen overnight. Even Billie Eilish — who was, literally, an overnight success — didn't reach Top 40 radio for two years. Communities, like all good things, take time to build.

But if you focus on the pillars of meaningful connection — on crafting shared context, perspectives, actions, and social ties — and if you hone the foundations of your artistry — through consistency, connections, and competence — you *can* build a community that matters.

Ultimately, while the tools and platforms will change, the formula for success is pretty simple. Create art. Use the art to bring people into your world. Engage with your community around your art.

And repeat.

This process can be financially viable. It's meaningful because we're made to connect with others. It's a ton of fun, too.

It's not used-car sales.

You'll need to figure out what you want your community to look like. You'll need to learn from others who have done it. You'll need to plan. You'll need to be smart with your tactics. Most of all, you'll need to be yourself.

I hope you're inspired to start, because the goal is worth the work of promotion. You'll get to make a living. You'll get to make music. You'll get to make friends.

You'll get to make a difference with a community you care about.

Here's to the good work of building it.

DOCUMENT INDEX

I list a lot of documents in this book. To help you keep them straight, here's everything I recommend that you create and basically live by as you work to promote your music.

Core Values List

What: This is a listing of 3-5 core values that will shape your perspective as an artist. These are the things you really care about, codified.

When: You should create this right away.

Where: This is discussed in detail in Chapter 6.

Community Visualization Plan

What: This is a document that defines the ideal characteristics of your community using the four pillars. This is your big-picture goal. It's the picture on the front of the puzzle box; it's the whole point of promotion.

When: You should create this right away.

Where: This is discussed in detail in Chapter 6.

3-2-1 Goal Plan

What: This is a document that contains your high-level community goal and your main goals for the next three months. You'll be

When: You should create this before you work on your next release.

Where: This is discussed in detail in Chapter 6.

Artist Impact List

What: This is a document that lists 10 artists you're similar to using feedback gathered from 10 people you know, 10 artists you aspire to be like, and 10 artists you'd like to work with.

When: You should create this before you work on your next release.

Where: This is discussed in detail in Chapter 6.

Platform Scorecard

What: This is a spreadsheet that tracks the most important number for each platform you use. It should be updated monthly and before each release cycle.

When: You should create this before you work on your next release.

Where: This is discussed in detail in Chapter 7.

Posting Playbook

What: This is a document that outlines your social media strategy. It should include 3-10 post types to help you more easily create social media content.

When: You should create this before you work on your next release.

Where: This is discussed in detail in Chapter 10.

EPK

What: This is a document that contains your artist bio, artist brief, a press release for your latest project, and links to relevant profiles. It will be sent to industry contacts.

When: You should create your bio now. You should create all other documents as you schedule your next release.

Where: This is discussed in detail in Chapter 14.

Press Tracking Sheet

What: This is a sheet that you'll use to track press campaigns as you work to secure a premiere.

When: You should create this as you work on a press campaign.

Where: This is discussed in detail in Chapter 15.

SOURCES

Expectations

1. Rosenzweig, M. (2020, February 03). Meet Billie Eilish, Pop's Next It Girl. Retrieved August 27, 2020, from https://www.vogue.com/article/billie-eilish-pops-next-it-girl
2. Stassen, M. (2019, December 17). Behind Billie Eilish: Meet the managers guiding the artist's global success. Retrieved August 27, 2020, from https://www.musicbusinessworldwide.com/behind-billie-eilish-meet-the-managers-guiding-the-artists-global-success/
3. Coscarelli, J. (2019, March 28). Billie Eilish Is Not Your Typical 17-Year-Old Pop Star. Get Used to Her. Retrieved August 27, 2020, from https://www.nytimes.com/2019/03/28/arts/music/billie-eilish-debut-album.html

3. The What and Why of Community

1. Macqueen, K. M., Mclellan, E., Metzger, D. S., Kegeles, S., Strauss, R. P., Scotti, R., . . . Trotter, R. T. (2001). What Is Community? An Evidence-Based Definition for Participatory Public Health. *American Journal of Public Health, 91*(12), 1929-1938. doi:10.2105/ajph.91.12.1929
2. Martin, M., & Watters, G. (2019, February 10). 'We Need To Exist In Multitudes': Noname Talks Artistic Independence, Women In Rap. Retrieved August 27, 2020, from https://www.npr.org/2019/02/10/692701998/we-need-to-exist-in-multitudes-noname-talks-artistic-independence-women-in-rap-a
3. Forget the beef with J. Cole – here's why Noname is an essential voice. (2020, June 19). Retrieved August 27, 2020, from https://www.nme.com/en_au/features/no-name-j-cole-snow-on-tha-bluff-book-club-chance-the-rapper-beef-cancelled-2691407
4. Hawley, L. (2017, November 28). Q A with Derek Webb. Retrieved August 27, 2020, from https://inallthings.org/qa-with-derek-webb/
5. Eells, J. (2020, August 05). Lil Nas X: Inside the Rise of a Hip-Hop Cowboy. Retrieved August 27, 2020, from https://www.rollingstone.com/music/music-features/lil-nas-x-old-town-road-interview-new-album-836393/
6. A Dream of John Ball, 1888. (n.d.). Retrieved August 27, 2020, from http://morrisedition.lib.uiowa.edu/dream1888text.html

4. Why Community Matters

1. Mcleod, S. (2020, March 20). Maslow's Hierarchy of Needs. Retrieved August 27, 2020, from https://www.simplypsychology.org/maslow.html
2. Brooks, D. (2020). *The second mountain: The quest for a moral life*. New York: Random House.
3. Krakauer, J. (2007). *Into the wild*. New York: Villard Books.
4. Kelly, K. (n.d.). 1,000 True Fans. Retrieved August 27, 2020, from https://kk.org/thetechnium/1000-true-fans/
5. U.S. Music Mid-Year Report 2019. (n.d.). Retrieved August 27, 2020, from https://www.nielsen.com/us/en/insights/report/2019/u-s-music-mid-year-report-2019/

5. The Foundations of Artistry

1. Spotify CEO talks Covid-19, artist incomes and podcasting (interview). (n.d.). Retrieved August 27, 2020, from https://musically.com/2020/07/30/spotify-ceo-talks-covid-19-artist-incomes-and-podcasting-interview/

8. Base Platform Setup

1. Plummer, M., Knight, R., Friedman, R., & Webb, C. (2019, March 21). How to Spend Way Less Time on Email Every Day. Retrieved August 27, 2020, from https://hbr.org/2019/01/how-to-spend-way-less-time-on-email-every-day
2. Aboulhosn, S. (2020, August 17). 18 Facebook statistics every marketer should know in 2020. Retrieved August 27, 2020, from https://sproutsocial.com/insights/facebook-stats-for-marketers/

9. Music Platform Setup

1. Spangler, T. (2020, February 05). Spotify Zooms to 124 Million Premium Subscribers in Q4, Record Quarterly Gain Driven by Promos. Retrieved August 27, 2020, from https://variety.com/2020/digital/news/spotify-q4-2019-premium-subscribers-podcast-investments-1203493393/
2. (n.d.). Retrieved August 27, 2020, from https://www.YouTube.com/about/press/

10. Social Platform Setup

1. Clement, J. (2020, July 24). Instagram: Age distribution of global audiences 2020. Retrieved August 27, 2020, from https://www.statista.com/statistics/325587/instagram-global-age-group/

The Strange Trail of Promotion

1. Perlroth, N. (2014, February 19). Meet Lord Huron, a Musical Project That Is Also an Alternate Reality Game. Retrieved August 27, 2020, from https://bits.blogs.nytimes.com/2014/02/19/meet-lord-huron-a-musical-project-that-is-also-an-alternate-reality-game/
2. [Exclusive] Read the First Four Pages of Lord Huron's Comic Book 'Strange Trails'. (n.d.). Retrieved August 27, 2020, from https://www.vice.com/en_us/article/qkwjgq/exclusive-read-the-first-four-pages-of-lord-hurons-comic-book-strange-trails

12. Promotion During Creation (Part I)

1. Leif Vollebekk On the Synesthesia Of His New Album 'Twin Solitude'. (n.d.). Retrieved August 27, 2020, from https://www.villagevoice.com/2017/02/23/leif-vollebekk-on-the-synesthesia-of-his-new-album-twin-solitude/
2. Alois, J. (2014, August 28). Crowdfunding 101: Kickstarter & Indiegogo (Infographic). Retrieved August 27, 2020, from https://www.crowdfundinsider.com/2014/08/47987-crowdfunding-101-kickstarter-indiegogo-infographic/

ABOUT THE AUTHOR

Jon's the founder of *Two Story Melody* (a music blog) and Two Story Media (a music PR firm).

Here are two truths and a lie about him: Jon loves understanding how songs are made. Jon once attempted to swim across the Pacific Ocean, but only made it to Hawaii. Jon was the stunt double for Sandra Bullock in the films *Gravity* and *The Blindside*.

Printed in Great Britain
by Amazon

77910711R00108